TESTIMONIALS

"This is a brilliant work! *Thinking Beyond the Obvious* is a simple, yet profound concept. When applied success expands exponentially."

KEN D. FOSTER
Author, Speaker, Coach

"*Thinking Beyond the Obvious* provides vital information that a business owner must keep in mind as they evaluate their daily operations and when they think about the future of their company. Fortunately, Robert has woven this simple concept into engaging, memorable stories that will keep these ideas alive and ready for use by every small business owner who reads this book."

BETH BRIDGES
Membership Director, Clovis Chamber of Commerce
The Networking Motivator™

"Robert Mano is among the very few who truly understands what it's like to own a small business. While others talk in business school rhetoric, he explains it in a way that we can easily understand."

DAVID LOCHER
Owner, Dashcorp Technology Group
CEO, Bridgecomm, Inc.

"*Thinking Beyond the Obvious* is an easy read and will inspire you to think and take action. Robert Mano has the credentials and integrity to help you position your business for success."

ROBERT HARLAN
Vice President, Comerica Bank

"*Thinking Beyond the Obvious* is an eye opener. It provides a simple to understand concept that is relevant to every business, big or small."

FRED L. FURROW
CEO, Full Circle Energy, Inc.

THINKING beyond THE OBVIOUS

ROBERT MANO

MORGAN JAMES PUBLISHING • NEW YORK

Copyright © 2011 Robert Mano

ISBN: 978-1-60037-869-0 (Paperback) / 978-1-60037-870-6 (EPub)
Library of Congress Control Number: 2010937001

Published by:
MORGAN JAMES PUBLISHING
The Entrepreneurial Publisher
5 Penn Plaza, 23rd Floor, New York City, New York 10001
(212) 655-5470 Office (516) 908-4496 Fax
www.MorganJamesPublishing.com

Cover/Interior Design by:
Rachel Lopez
rachel@r2cdesign.com

Disclaimer/Legal Information: The purpose of this book is to educate, inform and help the reader look at their business through more awakened and discerning eyes. Every effort has been made in this book to give credit where credit is due. Unfortunately, I have a slight dilemma, I have learned not only from my own personal experiences but from the experiences of others as well.

I have attended numerous seminars, listened to countless hours of webinars, listened to hour's worth of CD's from some of the most well respected consultants, trainers, coaches and speakers while driving. I have read numerous books, articles, magazines, newspapers, whitepapers, and periodicals over the years. Therefore the possibility exists that credit may not be given where credit is due. My intent is to give credit where due and I ask for forgiveness if I was remiss.

The author, Mano Y Mano Consulting and the publishing company Morgan James shall have neither liability nor responsibility to any person or business with respect to any losses or damages caused or alleged to be caused directly or indirectly by the information in this book. The intent of the author is only to offer information of a general nature to help you in your quest for business success. In the event you use any of the information in this book for you or your business, which is your constitutional right, the author and the publisher assume no responsibility for your actions or your success.

To my wife, Teresa,
for your continuous encouragement,
for your unyielding love, and for believing in me.

ACKNOWLEDGEMENTS

I t all started with a blank piece of paper, a proven secret that will position a business for success and a burning desire to share what I have learned with others. But a blank sheet of paper does not become a book without the help of others.

I have been blessed to have a number of people contribute to the book. First and foremost, my wife Teresa, without her support I would not have been able to write this book or live out my passion. She would encourage me everyday to stay the course and stay committed. I thank God everyday for giving me Teresa, my lifetime partner, to share both the challenging and joyous times we've had together.

I am very grateful for my mom, who at the age of 90 spent countless hours reading the initial manuscript and correcting my many mistakes. No matter how many times I proofed the copy, for some reason I couldn't catch every mistake. And for keeping an old picture of me holding the money I made from picking tomatoes— my first *Thinking Beyond the Obvious* moment.

I am very grateful to my mother-in-law Betty. When Teresa and I would visit, we would have very early morning conversations. I would share the ideas for the various chapters of the book and she would always have an insightful comment or an encouraging word.

I am grateful for my mastermind group and in particular I want to thank Beth Bridges who provided feedback and encouragement throughout the process. I want to thank Jill Hendrickson who meticulously read every chapter and provided editing assistance.

Finally, I want to recognize the contribution of the many businesses that despite not knowing provided the insight and the revelation of the *Thinking Beyond the Obvious* concept.

Most importantly I thank God for his guidance and direction and for the many middle of the night insights that I needed to get on paper before I would fall back asleep.

And finally for all my consulting and coaching clients who endured me continually stressing the importance of *Thinking Beyond the Obvious*.

CONTENTS

INTRODUCTION

You have just arrived home from a long day at work. Your wife, bless her heart, greets you with the welcoming hello kiss. You are totally exhausted, frustrated and disappointed that your business dream is no longer a dream but a nightmare you are living every day. You are not sure why. You are doing everything the business courses suggest, but to no avail. You start asking yourself the question, *"What am I missing?"*

As I listened to the frustrations expressed by business owners, executives and managers, trying to understand the whys of business, I began to realize they do not understand the key driving secret to business success.

Welcome to *Thinking Beyond the Obvious*. Whether you are a business owner, solopreneur, or an executive, *Thinking Beyond the Obvious* provides a simple concept that weaves through every successful business regardless of its size. I believe this simple concept will transform your business. To transform is "to change the nature, function or condition of..." Do you want to transform your business? Do you want to avoid the costly mistakes that can be made? And believe me they can be very costly. I should know. I learned the hard way.

Let me first take you back to about 10 years ago when this all began. I was president of a company that had sales of just under $150 million. That was up from $45 million when I first joined them. I was called into a meeting in San Francisco with a consultant representing the new owners. I had just spent the last year working with a major bank to help sell the company. I had put my heart and soul into developing the company while keeping the employees insulated from a potential buyout. And you guessed it, the new owners wanted to bring in their own management team and I was just fired. Our kids were in high school and the thought of uprooting them again was not an option. They had already moved twice at early ages.

My dilemma, California's San Joaquin Valley was not exactly a hotbed of corporate activity, and getting a new executive management position would require relocating. So what does a displaced executive do? He looks for an opportunity to go into business for himself and be his own boss. I looked at the various options. Selling life insurance, financial planning and one day I was looking in the want ads and saw a small ad for a fast food restaurant. I inquired and learned it consisted of three established franchise sandwich shops. I did my due diligence having just been through the exercise in my corporate position. I subsequently purchased two of the sandwich shops and followed that by opening a third. I thought I could use the skills I had acquired as a corporate president to manage the shops. The key was to use the skills I had acquired during my corporate career and that was something I did not do. If I had, those sandwich shops would have been successful. But I was a middle-aged executive who just took a tremendous blow to the ribs followed by a blow to the chin. I was knocked to the canvas, to use a boxing analogy, and did not pick myself up until a number of years later. During this time on the canvas I ignored what I had learned as a successful business executive. I did not implement the principles that had helped me achieve success in every management and executive position I held.

The critical learning from this, besides what is forthcoming in the eight chapters of this book is, if you are the owner of a business you must love your work. It needs to be your passion. These sandwich shops were not my passion. I went from being a corporate president to making sandwiches and cleaning toilets. Yes, I would clean the toilets, because no matter how many times I would show the employees that the toilets were not clean, they just couldn't get them cleaned to my satisfaction. We will talk about that later.

I wasn't really sure what my passion was. My corporate career was just something you did when you graduated from college. Although I worked hard and quickly advanced up the corporate ladder, I never stopped to discover what it was I really wanted to do. After all, I was making excellent money and Teresa and I had pretty much whatever we wanted. Nice home, Lake House, new cars, a classic car. But what I didn't have was that sense of satisfaction that I was accomplishing what I wanted in life. I hadn't yet discovered my "why?"

The sandwich shops were not my passion and when you own your own business and it is not your passion; your business will suck both the life out of you as well as impact you financially. Is your business your passion?

Five years later I ended up walking away from the stores. I sold some of the equipment and took a financial bath. And I mean a financial bath. We lost both homes, we were driving an older car and I was driving my classic car. But what could have been regarded as a defeat turned out to be the best thing that could have happened. It led me to my passion. My passion is to take what I have learned and what I discovered and assist small businesses in maximizing their potential. My passion is to help business owners avoid some of the costly mistakes I made. To quote noted author Brian Tracy, "No one lives long enough to learn everything they need to learn starting from scratch. To be successful, we absolutely, positively have to find the people who have already paid the price to learn the things that we need to achieve our goals."

I read what seemed like every business book written, listened to countless hours of CDs, attended workshops, attended numerous online webinars hosted by a number of very successful consultants and reflected back on what I had done in my very successful corporate career. It was during this process I discovered the *Thinking Beyond the Obvious* concept. As I observed what successful businesses were doing, I recognized what I believe to be the secret to a successful business. This book will illuminate the basic concept and give you examples of what has worked for me as well as provide you examples of what successful companies are doing to guarantee that you are successful too. I want you to avoid the costly mistakes that I made. My passion is to use my past experiences, good or bad, to guide you through the maze of underachievement, confusion and misguided direction to position your business for unrivaled success. I want you to discover the key driving factors in business and use them to transform your business. I am passionate about sharing with you what I have learned.

Nothing is ever perfect; you may have some setbacks along the way. But do not let them overwhelm you. As my mother in-law Betty Holly says. *"Life's lessons are the building blocks to the future."*

Thinking Beyond the Obvious will illuminate a key foundational concept that I believe drives successful businesses. You will quickly recognize this foundational concept, in fact, you will recognize it in every successful business. *Thinking Beyond the Obvious* will lead you to see each successful business, including your own through a completely different and more awakened pair of eyes. Understanding and applying the *Thinking Beyond the Obvious* concept will:

- Help you differentiate your business from every other business in the marketplace by recognizing what other successful businesses are doing and successfully implementing those strategies in your business.

- Help you position your business for success by providing simple, proven ideas that you can immediately use.

- Transform your attitude into one of "Wow!" "I can do this."

Through the pages of this book, we will explore the basic foundational concept of *Thinking Beyond the Obvious* and seven areas of your business where the *Thinking Beyond the Obvious* concept needs to be applied. I will use simple-to-follow illustrations from my own personal experience to illuminate the point. I will also illustrate practices others have used to underscore the simple concept. These examples will allow you to experience what others have done. The illustrations will help you paint a mental picture and bring life to the concepts discussed. These concepts are valuable insights that are sprinkled throughout each chapter.

A *Thinking Beyond the Obvious Success Action Guide*, with accompanying CD's, is available to help train you to Think Beyond the Obvious. The guide teaches you through an intuitive process how you can implement these valuable *Thinking Beyond the Obvious* insights in your business today. It is implementing these insights that will differentiate your business from your competitors, making it more successful despite competing in the same external environment as every other business.

It has been said numerous times, do what you always do and you will get what you always got. Another way to look at this is, do what ordinary businesses do and you will get the same ordinary results. As Stephen M.R. Covey in his book the *"The Speed of Trust"* proposes, *"Change the way you see will automatically change what you do and the results you get."*

The next steps are entirely yours; put on your *Thinking Beyond the Obvious* glasses, finish reading the book and discover the simple concept that drives successful businesses. And lastly, look for ways that you can position your business for success by *Thinking Beyond the Obvious*. Because if you do not change the way you view things even after reading this book, your results will not change.

CHAPTER ONE

Picking Tomatoes
My First Thinking Beyond the Obvious Moment

I can remember as a thirteen year old living in Santa Clara, California, yes the Silicon Valley, before the tremendous growth explosion. There were still fruit orchards and vegetable farms. That summer I was looking for a way to earn a little extra money. As I was riding with my dad from the hardware store, we passed by a tomato farm and posted was a sign, Wanted Tomato Pickers, start Monday. I can remember telling my dad I was going to be there early Monday morning. A friend and I started out early that Monday morning. We rode our bikes to the farm that was probably 3–4 miles away. We were both given two buckets, those large five gallon buckets that usually have paint in them, assigned a row and given a card which was punched for each bucket returned full. We quickly filled our first two buckets and this is when the difficulty began. Those buckets were heavy, and while most of the men easily carried two buckets to the dumping station, I could barely carry one. The money was made in filling the buckets, not spending all your time trying to carry the buckets to the dumping station. When you returned to the station, they punched your card and gave you replacement buckets, which in my case was just one. By the way, we were paid $.10 per bucket and the good field workers were filling 25 to 30 buckets an hour. I was struggling to carry the bucket; I had to drag it along the dirt to get it to the dumping station. Well this was not working, so I began to ponder a way that I could make it work for me.

The next day, before we went back to continue to pick tomatoes, I tied my red radio flyer wagon to my bike. Now I wasn't carrying the buckets but pulling them in my wagon. And you know what? I could get two buckets in the wagon. It was sure easier than trying to carry one bucket at a time. I had found a solution that was outside the boundaries of ordinary thinking. Without even knowing it, I had started *Thinking Beyond the Obvious*. By the way, we picked tomatoes for 3 days and made $25.00. Not bad for a scrawny thirteen year old. In fact the $25.00 was about what you would have made at the time for 3 days work if you were paid minimum wage, which was $1.25 per hour.

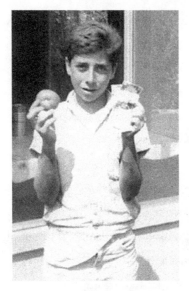

Money made from picking tomatoes

What does picking tomatoes have to do with transforming your business? Read on to discover how what I learned "picking tomatoes" is an important key to the success of business today.

"But we've never done it that way before." Have you heard yourself saying that to others? Have you caught yourself saying those words to your employees? Nothing stifles a business more quickly than those words. You are so caught up in the way you are currently doing things that you are blind to new ideas. Maybe it is a fear of failure or maybe it is the fear of the unknown. Maybe it is the fear of trying something new. Whatever the reason, those thoughts are stifling your business. Fear will cause you to avoid change and not take action, and the only way to drive away fear is to take action. As a business owner, executive, or manager you can not be afraid to make changes, to look for ways to improve, to look for solutions that are outside the boundaries of ordinary thinking. You must learn to *Think Beyond the Obvious*.

In business today, regardless of where you are, there are a number of things that must be done in order to give you or your business a chance of being successful. We will call these the obvious. The obvious is completing your responsibilities with excellence. The obvious is completing an annual business plan. And it doesn't have to be the detailed plan they teach in business school. Many times it is simply answering a few pointed questions. The obvious is monitoring sales and expenses. All seem fairly obvious, but you would be surprised how many businesses do not have a simple plan or how many have employees that do not uphold to their responsibilities. But this is not what differentiates businesses. Doing the obvious will only allow your business to compete in today's business environment. The obvious is doing what everyone else is doing because you think that because they are doing it, it must be the right thing to do.

This book is not a how-to-do the obvious book. If you are not doing the obvious, stop reading and take the time you would spend reading this book and complete the obvious. Think of what you are doing everyday and insure that you are doing the obvious well. Once you have the obvious in order, be prepared to learn how to think beyond the obvious. *Thinking Beyond the Obvious* is recognizing and applying solutions that are outside the boundaries of ordinary thinking, solutions that will position your business for success.

Thinking Beyond the Obvious is not thinking outside the box. We have all heard that you need to think outside the box. Thinking outside the box may lead you astray. There is nothing wrong with being inside the box. Think of a box as playing field. You are about to play a football game on the field. Thinking outside the box could have you playing on the wrong field or even in the wrong game. *Thinking Beyond the Obvious* would have you playing on the same field but playing in such a way that it is beyond the ordinary. One of the greatest football coaches of all time, Bill Walsh, was called an offensive genius. He developed a system that was beyond the obvious. Bill created and implemented the West Coast offense that completely changed the offensive structure of football today. Bill played within the same box or on the same field, but one of his difference makers was the West Coast offense. I am not saying that is the only reason, because he did have some Hall of Fame players in Joe Montana, Steve Young, Jerry Rice and Ronnie Lott.

The difference maker that enabled Bill Walsh as a coach of the San Francisco 49er's to win multiple Super Bowls or myself as a scrawny thirteen year old to make $25.00 "picking tomatoes" was finding a solution that was outside the boundaries of ordinary thinking.

Thinking Beyond the Obvious is playing on the right field and looking for solutions that are outside the boundaries of ordinary thinking. Applying the *Thinking Beyond the Obvious* concept will differentiate your business from every other business in the marketplace. Applying the *Thinking Beyond the Obvious* concept will position your business for success. Intuitively understanding the *Thinking Beyond the Obvious* concept will transform your attitude into one of "Wow, I can do this."

It has been said numerous times, do what you have always done and you will get what you always got. Another way to look at this is, do what ordinary businesses have done and you will get the same ordinary results. Do what ordinary individuals do and you will be just like them.

Are you ready to change the way you see things? Are you ready to positively impact your business? Are you ready to take your business to the next level?

Sometimes a concept when only presented in words is difficult to understand. We have all read a page from a book or a column and thought what did I just read? Many times you will reread the page thinking you might have dozed off. The old saying a picture is worth a thousand words is so true. In this case, I will try to paint a mental picture of the *Thinking Beyond the Obvious* concept through the use of numerous examples. Each example illustrates the *Thinking Beyond the Obvious* concept. They represent completely different industries or completely different periods in history, but all illustrating the *Thinking Beyond the Obvious* concept. All are relevant to the premise and all will help you create that mental picture, that intuitive understanding of what it means to *Think Beyond the Obvious*—an understanding that will change the way you look at every business, yours included, an understanding that will allow you to play on the same field or within the same box, but now in a way that could be the difference maker.

Once you intuitively understand the basic premise of *Thinking Beyond the Obvious*, you will begin to see the concept manifested in businesses everywhere. You will look at businesses and immediately recognize a way the business is operating that represents *Thinking Beyond the Obvious*.

Thinking Beyond the Obvious Examples

Ever stop and think about how some things were invented? Sometimes it just takes innovation, which is looking for that solution that is outside the boundaries of ordinary thinking or applying a new idea or concept to solve a real world problem. Take for example something as simple as the pocket in your pants. Someone had to *Think Beyond the Obvious*. This has been going on throughout history. Back to the pocket, sometime in the 1700's, pockets as we know them today were developed. But ours are very different from an early form of pockets; the early form was a small bag or purse hung from one's belt or even around one's neck. Easy target for what we today call the "grab and run."

In order to make it difficult for the "grab and run" thief, pockets were then hung from the belt on the inside of the clothes rather than the outside. Can you imagine having to unbutton your shirt or pants to get into your pocket? Well what do you think they did? They cut a slit in the side of the pants to get into the pocket but trying to open the pocket through a slit in the pants was difficult to say the least? Someone suggested sewing the pocket right inside the slit in the pants so that one's hand went directly into the pocket. Someone had the insight to *Think Beyond the Obvious*. (http://www.bbc.co.uk/dna/h2g2/ A798159.)

On February 26, 1829 a Jewish boy named Loeb Straus was born in Buttenheim, Germany. As a young man Loeb changed his name to Levi and immigrated to San Francisco. It's where he opened a textile company. One day a gold miner walked into Levi's shop and confronted the young merchant. "Look at these," said the miner pointing to his pants. "I bought 'em six months ago and now they're full of holes!" When Levi asked why, the miner explained, "We work on our knees most of the time."

"What you need is some really strong material," replied Levi. "We have some canvas, I'm sure they won't get holes." A tailor was called; the miner had a new set of trousers. Soon miners across the west were wearing Levi Straus's jeans. (Stephen Van Dulkin, Inventing the 19th Century: 100 Inventions That Shaped the Victorian Age, from Aspirin to the Zeppelin. New York: New York University, 2001, pg32). Those were both examples from early history but following is a more recent example.

Ever wonder how post-it notes were developed. The 3M Company encourages creativity from its employees. The company allows its researchers to spend part of their time on projects that interest them. Many times a spark of an idea has turned into a successful product that has boosted 3M's profits tremendously. Some years ago a scientist named Art Fry came up with an idea for one of 3M's best selling products. Art was frustrated every Sunday as he sang in the church choir. After marking his pages in the hymnal with small bits of paper that always fell out, an idea suddenly struck him. He remembered an adhesive developed by an associate that everyone thought was a failure because it did not stick very well. "I coated the adhesive on a paper sample," Fry recalls and found that it was not only a good book mark but great for writing notes. "It will stay in place as long as you want it to, and then you can remove it without damage." The resulting product was called Post-it and is one of 3M's most successful office products. One year after its introduction Post-it Notes were named 3M's outstanding new products. 3M employed a strategy that is covered in greater detail in the *Fruitful Employee* chapter.

The *Thinking Beyond the Obvious* concept is also evident in both good economics times as well as times when individuals may be struggling. Although the current economic environment has put additional pressures on businesses to succeed, success can still be manifested by looking for solutions that are outside the boundaries of ordinary thinking. Charles B. Darrow of Germantown, Pennsylvania in 1934 following the stock market crash of 1929 had an idea for a board game. He took the game to the executives at Parker Brothers, a company almost driven out of business by the Great Depression. Darrow called the game *"Monopoly ®,"* but Parker Brothers rejected it because of "52 design errors." Undaunted Darrow looked for a solution. With the help of a printer friend, Darrow produced five thousand handmade sets and sold them to a Philadelphia department store where the game became an overnight sensation. In 1935, Parker Brothers reconsidered and began producing the game. Since then an estimated 500 million people from around the world have played *"Monopoly®"* Ironic that a game about investing and living in luxury was introduced during a time of financial strafe. Parker Brothers went into around-the-clock production and sold 20,000 sets per week when it was first introduced. (http://www. hasbro.com/monopoly)

Can you imagine seeing with your tongue? That is truly *Thinking Beyond the Obvious* but for Roger Behm it was a reality. Roger Behm lost his sight at the age of sixteen as a result of an inherited disease that destroyed the retinas in his eyes. However, part of his world is coming back into focus through experimental technology called BrainPort. Roger places a device over his head, turns it on and once again he was able to discern light and dark, shapes and shadows, letters, numbers and even a rolling golf ball. It works by converting images from a video camera to electrical impulses that are transmitted via the tongue to the brain of the blind person and turned again into black and white images that the user sees. It takes advantage of groundbreaking work or, what

I call *Thinking Beyond the Obvious*, by a University of Wisconsin-Madison scientist.

Erik Weihenmayer has tested the device under more trying circumstances. He is the only blind man to reach the summit of Mt. Everest. He has used the device to help him hike in the woods, ascend climbing walls, play tic-tac-toe with his daughter or simply pet the family dog. The gear was invented by Paul Back-y-Rita a neuroscientist at the University of Wisconsin, Madison. Back-y-Rita has devoted much of his career to a single revolutionary concept that senses are interchangeable. All I can say is "Wow."

Thinking Beyond the Obvious strategies at times do not have to be profound innovative solutions. At times they can be a simple way of handling a customer. I was recently reading a letter to the editor column in our local newspaper. The writer took his clock to a local clock shop to be fixed. The man who helped him showed him it was a simple problem and fixed it right on the spot. The owner of the clock asked the service person how much he owed for the repair and he said nothing. The man who helped him could have easily charged him for his services. Charging for the repair is probably what most ordinary companies would have done. But in this instance the clock shop employee did what most would not; he did not charge him for the repair. He gained a customer that became an evangelist for the clock shop. This will be discussed in greater detail in the *Fruitful Employees* chapter.

This brings me to home remodeling. With the influx of home remodeling programs, Teresa and I would sometimes tackle a room renovation. We actually work extremely well together. They say if you can work on a home project together your marriage has a greater chance of success. Teresa and I decided we would convert one of the kid's bedrooms into a home office. No, we did not kick the kids out of their rooms, all of our kids are now young adults living on their own. It all started with a trip to the home improvement store to purchase the paint. The first challenge is lifting the gallons out of the cart and into your car. Those wire handles are uncomfortable as they press into the palm of your hands.

Usually the painting mess starts as soon as you try to pry open the can with a screwdriver. How many times have you spilled paint on the floor before you even pour it into the tray? Or once you do pour it into the tray, the paint drips down the side of the can. You wipe the paint with your brush only to paint over the cleaning and drying instructions. Try putting the lid back on and resealing, you better put a rag over the top because when you take your hammer and pound the lid back on, if you didn't, you will have paint splattered everywhere.

So consider a bright idea from Dutch Boy, paint containers made of recyclable plastic with a side handle and a Twist & Pour spout. The new easy pour plastic gallon containers have plenty of advantages. They weigh less, will not dent or rust and are easy to open and reclose. In 2002 The Dutch Boy group introduced the new Twist & Pour ™ paint container.

It became an instant consumer favorite and won numerous awards. Dutch Boy, a unit of the Cleveland base Sherwin-Williams Company, had been working on the new paint can, an all plastic gallon container with a twist off lid and easy pour spout for a couple of years. There were complications along the way, the company had to deal with production challenges, the original paint can was metal and the conveyor belts were magnetic, designed for the metal can. The in-store paint shakers had to be retrofitted to accommodate the new plastic container. But all in all the introduction has been a success because someone at The Dutch Boy Group looked for a solution that was outside the boundaries of ordinary thinking. And not only did they find a solution, they did not let production and retail challenges stop them.

The following example demonstrates how even your advertising can use the *Thinking Beyond the Obvious* concept. When Kentucky Fried Chicken (KFC) was looking for a way to introduce their new *Fiery Grilled Wings*, they looked for creative solutions that were outside the boundaries of ordinary thinking. Instead of buying more billboards, KFC was truly *Thinking Beyond the Obvious* when they used their marketing dollars, specifically their advertising dollars, to refurbish old fire hydrants, fire extinguishers and smoke detectors in public buildings in exchange for the ability to brand the equipment to promote the new *Fiery Grilled Wings*. The accompanying letter to city mayors from the president of KFC is implementing the *Thinking Beyond the Obvious* concept.

Louisville, KY – Business Wire 1–6–2010

January 6, 2010

Dear Mayor:

As you know first hand, city budgets across the country are under fire as leaders are forced to make tough decisions about how to assign limited public funding. Often these tight budgets make funding for public services such as fire safety and prevention more difficult to come by.

Add to this the fact that in 2008 property loss due to fires was estimated at $15.5 billion and that January is the peak month for residential fires and the topic of fire safety really starts to heat up as it gets cold across the country.

All of this has the KFC Colonel and his crew fired up to improve America's safety. In honor of our new Fiery Grilled Wings, we are offering fire safety improvements, via fire hydrant repairs or fire extinguisher replacements for communities across the country. And, because the Colonel has become an expert on all things fiery with the introduction of KFC's new Fiery Grilled Wings, he'll provide his stamp of approval on each and every hydrant or extinguisher he replaces or helps repair.

Is your city feeling the heat? We invite you to tell us why we should help you extinguish the problem in your community. KFC will be accepting funding requests until January 28 and will announce the winning cities shortly after.

KFC has been bringing communities together around the dinner table for more than 50 years. We invite you and your city to become a part of a new tradition and accept our offer to help improve fire safety in your city. Together, we can provide a safer winter for your community.

Sincerely,
Roger Eaton
President of KFC

The *Thinking Beyond the Obvious* concept is not just limited to business. It also applies to athletics. Remember the stifling words, *"But we have never done it that way before."* Prior to 1968 high jumpers would use the straddle technique or scissors jump to clear the high jump bar. Dick Fosbury was a struggling high jumper. He was inconsistent using the more conventional techniques of the 1950's and 1960's. Dick Fosbury began practicing a unique approach (outside the boundaries of ordinary thinking) to jumping over the high jump bar.

Dick Fosbury began approaching the bar with his back to it and jumping over the bar horizontally. He completed the jump with his back arched looking upward and his arms at his side. Can you imagine what others were thinking when they first saw Dick jump the bar backwards and looking up? I am sure they were saying that will never work, we have never done it that way! Dick Fosbury won the gold medal in the high jump in the 1968 Summer Olympics and the Fosbury-flop, so appropriately named, is the dominant style used by high jumpers today.

As I look back over my career, example after example began to surface. My first real career job out of school was with the Nestle Company. I was hired as a sales representative. I had just completed my two weeks of training. The first two weeks were spent with another sales representative who was responsible for your training. All that was involved those first two weeks was following him around and observing and listening to what he did and how he did it. The second two weeks were spent in your own territory with your area manager. You were now responsible for mapping out your daily route, and that was prior to MapQuest. During the second week of training, I could remember waiting in the waiting room of the buyer and owner of a small five-store chain of grocery stores. When it was my turn, I looked to my area manager with that OK let's go look and he said "no you're ready; you can do it on your own". I went into the buyer's office, introduced myself and sat on the other side of what was the largest desk I had ever seen. The large desk was the buyer's way of intimidating and keeping sales reps at bay. As I was presenting the materials to him, I was struggling to read the brochure. It was a beautiful brochure created by the marketing department. It was just difficult to read upside-down.

On a side note; when you create a sales brochure, make sure the print is large enough so that you can read it upside-down. I

call this the *"upside-down rule"* of creating marketin.
Back to the sales call, as I was struggling to present the m.
upside down, I got up from my side of the desk and procee
to go around to his side of the desk. The buyer looked at me
with a look of amazement. "Young man what are you doing?"
He asked. "No one has ever come around from the other side of
the desk." I thought to myself uh-oh "I blew it." I simply said,
"I can't present upside down and I want to make sure I cover all
the material."

He looked up at me and said. "You got #%$^, put together a
truckload order for each store and when you're done, just come
back in and I will sign them." As I returned to the lobby, I had
a grin from ear to ear. My area manager asked me "How did it
go?" I said, "Fine, I guess. He just gave me an open order for 5
truckloads of product—one for each store." Later, when back in
the car, I asked my area manager why he had not made the call
with me. His response was, "He is the toughest buyer you will ever
face, especially for new sales reps." I think differently. I think my
area manager was afraid of him and just didn't want to experience
his wrath. The buyer remembered me each time I would call on
him. He would simply say, "I like you, you have @#$%. Just write
up the orders." Point here, I differentiated myself from every other
sales rep that called on him, I didn't realize it at the time but I was
Thinking Beyond the Obvious. And a postscript: within two years
the area manager ended up working for me as I was promoted to
area manager and he was subsequently demoted. A couple of years

CHAPTER ONE Picking Tomatoes...

ater I was transferred within Nestle to a marketing position in White Plains, New York.

While I was working for Nestle in their marketing department of the Chocolate Division, we all learned the story of Ruth Wakefield and the discovery of chocolate chip cookies. It all began in 1930 in Ruth's Massachusetts home. Her home was a haven to weary travelers between Boston and New York. Travelers would stop to enjoy the home cooked meals Ruth baked for her guests along with butter drop cookies, a favorite recipe dating back to the colonial days. One day Ruth cut a bar of Nestle® Semi-Sweet Chocolate into tiny bits and added them to her cookie dough. What was she thinking? By now you should know the answer. Much to her surprise the chocolate did not melt. In fact the chocolate held its shape and softened to a creamy texture. The resulting cookie became extremely popular at the Inn. Ruth's recipe was published in a Boston newspaper as well as other newspapers in the surrounding area. Eventually the recipe was printed on the wrapper of the Semi-Sweet Chocolate Bar. As the popularity of the cookie grew, Nestle looked for ways to make it easier for people to bake. First they scored the chocolate bar and packed it with a special chopper to ease the cutting into small pieces. In 1939 Nestle offered tiny pieces of chocolate in convenient ready-to-use packages. (Nestle Website).

To this day Nestle Tollhouse cookies are still my favorite cookie. I also remember that Nestle were continuously looking for ways to increase the usage of Nestle Semi-Sweet morsels.

Usage during the summer months declined. People did not want to turn the oven on for a prolonged period of time to bake batches of Tollhouse Cookies, hence the introduction of the pan cookie. The pan cookie is more like a brownie but still has the rich flavor of Traditional Tollhouse Cookies and yet it takes only 20–25 minutes to bake.

Nestle also experimented with using morsels in various cake recipes. While the morsels worked in cookies or the pan cookie, they didn't really work in cakes. The morsels would sink to the bottom of the cake pan due to their weight. Nestle looked for a *Thinking Beyond the Obvious* solution which led to the development of mini-morsels which were smaller in size and the morsels stayed suspended in the cake.

By now you have read a number of examples of businesses and individuals applying the *Thinking Beyond the Obvious* concept. Hopefully, you have a clear mental picture of what it means to *Think Beyond the Obvious*. Now look around at the successful businesses you know. Do what they are doing. Think beyond the obvious.

Over the next seven chapters we will explore key areas of business and thoughts on how you can apply the *Thinking Beyond the Obvious* concept. No chapter is all inclusive; there may be many other ways to apply the concept, but, if you will think beyond the obvious and apply the lessons within each chapter, you will position your business for success.

CHAPTER TWO

An Infected Workplace

Each and everyday, as we live our lives, there is one very valuable asset that costs us nothing. It is absolutely free and you are in control of it. That one asset is your attitude. Your attitude is not only one of your greatest personal assets; your attitude is also one of your greatest business assets. Your attitude serves as the lens through which you view your circumstance. When you turn your attitude over to your circumstances, you lose control over your ability to impact others. You lose control over your ability to both see and think beyond the obvious. When you turn your attitude over to your circumstances, it is reflected in both your actions and your words. Are there times when you can just sense in someone that something is bothering them? Maybe it's a death in the family or a heavy burden that they are carrying. You can sense it because it is being reflected in their voice or it is being reflected in their body language. It is being reflected in their attitude. They are just not their normal self. If you can sense it, don't you also think that your business associates, fellow employees or customers, and clients can also sense it?

What are your words projecting? What is your body language projecting? Are your words creating positive energy or are they creating negative energy? Is your body language projecting a positive flow or is your body language projecting a negative flow? The differences between the two can greatly affect your business. S. Clement W. Stone, a noted businessman and self-help book author says, *"There is little difference in people, but that little difference makes a big difference. The little difference is attitude. The big difference is whether it is positive or negative."*

Your Attitude

Attitude is the one thing you control. No one else can control your attitude nor can any one else force their attitude on you. Your attitude is an individual choice that can only be made by you. You and you alone determine your attitude. Jim Rome, noted motivational speaker, said, *"You must take personal responsibility. You cannot change the circumstances, the seasons, or the wind, but you can change yourself. That is something you have charge of. In order to change yourself you must change your attitude."*

Your attitude frames both your world and how others will see your world. Imagine you just met with the photographer to pick up the family portraits. You hadn't had a family portrait done since the kids were little. Now that they are older but still living at home, you thought this would be a good time to have a new family picture taken. The portrait was amazing. The photographer captured the essence of your family. You left the studio thinking, "I do not have a frame to place this picture in." Would you place the picture in an old, tattered and scratched frame? If you did, wouldn't it be harder to recognize and appreciate the beauty of the portrait? No, you would look for and purchase a beautiful new frame that would enhance the picture. In the same way that that picture frame can enhance or detract from the picture, your attitude has the same impact on what people see. Your attitude will impact how people see you. You will either attract people by your attitude or repel people by your attitude.

Your attitude also says a lot about who you really are. Your attitude is one of the leading factors that will either draw people toward you or turn them away. My mother-in-law, Betty Holly, is a living example of how an attitude can influence others. She always, and I mean always, has a positive attitude. It is one trait that my wife Teresa has inherited. Even when Betty was struggling through a marriage with an alcoholic husband or assisting him when he was bedridden, I never saw her waiver from her positive, hopeful attitude. And Betty's attitude is contagious; you can't help but feel the positive energy when you are around her. Wherever she goes, whether it's to the grocery store, the gas station or the hair salon, her positive, infectious attitude greatly affects everyone that she comes in contact with. Her genuine smile radiates and captures everyone around her. You see her attitude reflected through her words and her actions. In the same way your attitude frames the world around you. It affects how people respond to you.

Do not underestimate the genuineness of a smile, the sincerity of a touch or a hug, the power of the spoken word, the empathy of a sympathetic ear or the impact of an honest compliment or encouraging word.

When my daughter Alicia, was getting ready to move again, I would always remind her that her attitude would effect how well the move went. Her husband Joe is a Marine and his attitude is not always the most positive. I would always remind her of the story of the couple that was moving into a new city. They stopped at a gas station just outside the city to ask for directions, (must have been the wife who wanted to stop because men do not usually stop until they know they are lost). Once she received the directions she asked the gentleman who happened to be the owner what was the new city like. He answered with a question? "What was it like where you lived before?" Her answer was, "Everyone was so rude. The neighbors were loud. It was a very unfriendly town. I couldn't make any new friends. The school where my kids attended was horrible; my kids were not learning anything." His answer to her was, "That's pretty much the way it is here ma'am."

They went off on their way. Shortly after that another couple pulled up in a moving van. They were just moving into town and stopped to get gas. They were friendly and engaging. While they were buying sodas and snack for their kids, the mom asked the gentleman behind the counter, who once again happened to be the owner, "What's this community like?" And he answered once again with a question. "What was it like where you are coming from?" She responded, "We just loved it. Everyone was so friendly. We got to know our neighbors and they helped us get settled in. My kids loved school and the teachers were so concerned about how they were doing. My husband was transferred, if not, we would still be there." The gentleman looked at her and said, "Ma'am you'll find this city much like your last."

Two couples, with two different attitudes, both moving into the same city. I would venture to say the couple that had the negative attitude and the negative experience from where they were moving would have the same experience in the new city. The couple that had the positive experiences which was driven by their positive attitude would have the same positive experience in the new city. It is a matter of perception. You will find things to be just the way you think they are.

Our daughter, Alicia, took this to heart and had been extremely positive about their move to of all places Biloxi, Mississippi. Her overall experience had been extremely positive and I believe it all has to do with her attitude.

To *Think Beyond the Obvious* is to maintain a positive attitude in all you do—an attitude of expectancy, an attitude that good will come out of your circumstances. It is much easier to get wrapped up in the negative. It is what you read in the newspaper or hear on the news every day. There is a simple reason for that: Yellow Press sells. Newspapers are in the business of selling papers, and news programs are in the business of increasing viewership. The more viewers, the more news programs can charge for their advertising. Imagine you are in line at the grocery store. You look at two newspaper headlines that are right next to each other. The first reads, *"Beautiful Weather in the Days Ahead."* Would that headline motivate you to purchase the newspaper? Probably not. The second headline reads, *"Prepare for the Worst Storm in History."* Would that get your attention? Which paper would you be most likely to purchase? I would venture to say the latter.

An Infected Workplace

Do you want your workplace to be infected? Most people would say absolutely not before they even ask the question, "infected with what?" To be infected means to be contaminated with a disease-producing matter or to affect as if by a contagion. It also means to spread as an influence or emotional state. Wouldn't you want your workplace to be infected by that contagion if that contagion was a positive attitude? Imagine employees, customers and clients all being exposed to and infected by this contagion. Just like the flu or a cold can be passed along by contact, so can this contagion. No need to use the hand sanitizer, no need to wipe the grocery cart handle from fear of getting it. This contagion is passed from employee to employee, employee to customers and clients, and from customers to their contacts.

The contagion is your attitude and the attitude of your employees. What can you do, what steps can you take to infect your workplace? Can you imagine an infected workplace where no quarantine is needed? A workplace when as soon as a client or customer enters the door they are exposed to the positive attitude contagion. A simple smile is a place to start. It is an important element of creating an infected work place—a smile by the receptionist, by the hostess in a restaurant, or the customer service associate they do not even see.

I can remember my days as National Sales Manager of a Dried Fruit company. I had the customer service department reporting to me. They were responsible for handling the customer's as well as following-up with the customers upon shipment. These were the days before CRM systems. I can remember calling the customer service manager into my office one day. I wanted to create an infectious attitude and I instructed him to go to the store and purchase vanity mirrors to place next to each customer service associate's phone. I asked each associate to look into the mirror and smile as they were answering the phone. It is extremely difficult to be negative or have a negative attitude with a smile on your face. I would later come in contact with the customers and they would volunteer, "You have the friendliest customer service associates, it's like I can feel the radiance of their smile through the phone." I would just chuckle to myself.

How do you create that positive attitude in the workplace despite what the individual may be experiencing in the environment outside their work? First you must recognize the impact your attitude has on the workplace. Try it some time. Walk into your place of work and to everyone you meet or pass, say, "Wow, great day isn't?" You may begin to hear the gossip circulating like wildfire through the facility or office, "Boy what's going on" or "What's wrong with the boss? I haven't seen him or her in a mood like this before."

Or hum an upbeat song as you're walking through the halls or through the production facility. Before you know it, you'll begin to hear others also humming the song. You are beginning to spread the positive attitude contagion throughout the facility. Your simple words and your simple actions are the beginning of spreading the positive attitude contagion throughout the office or your place of work. *Think Beyond the Obvious*. Are there ways within your business that you can affect the attitude of those around you?

Attitude Adjustment

There are a number of ways that you can change the attitude of your employees which will change the attitude of your customers. First it starts with your own attitude. We have covered this in detail above and with the examples given but here are some more suggestions.

Show appreciation. Whether at home or at work, people want to feel appreciated. Sometimes it just takes a simple word of thanks. When was the last time you dropped someone a card saying how much you appreciate them. Do you ever get a simple thought, a prompting, that you should drop someone a note or send them a card? SendOutCards is building a significant business by helping people react to those promptings. With SendOutCards you can send a personalized card with a message you create, you can use your own handwriting and sign it with your own signature. You can send an individualized card through the mail without going to the local store to pick out a card - all for less than $2.00 per card and that includes the stamp. All from the convenience of a computer. SendOutCards is a rapidly growing business that was created by an individual wanting to react to those promptings and send a personal card. Let me take a moment here to relate the SendOutCards Story. It's the story of Kody Bateman, an individual who was driven to think beyond the obvious.

Everyone can recall an instance when they experienced a prompting—the strong need to act—but didn't. Kody Bateman is no exception, except that he took an ignored prompting and turned it into a successful company and a philosophy for a successful life. Years ago Kody ignored a prompting to say goodbye to his older brother when he was moving across the country. He just waved good-bye as opposed to giving his brother a big hug. Two months later, Kody received the tragic news that his brother had been killed in an unfortunate work related accident. From that day forward, Kody promised to act on his promptings and to help others to do the same. The experience led Kody on a twenty-year journey to help himself and others act on their promptings. The SendOutCards business he created lets people do just that by sending greeting cards and gifts to family and friends, building relationships and forging bonds. (Promptings Website)

Kody started his SendOutCards business with a simple thought, something that hadn't been done in the greeting card industry before. SendOutCards is an amazing system that is outside the boundaries of ordinary thinking. SendOutCards is a great relationship-building tool that businesses can use to follow-up with prospects and customers. It is a way in which you can positively affect someone's attitude. I have used it to provide an encouraging or congratulatory word. In more than one instance, I have had friends or associates thank me for the encouraging word I sent them via a personalized card. If you would like to learn more about SendOutCards go to: http://www.sendoutcards.com/manoymano.

Celebrate along the way. Recognize personal milestones, business milestones, personal accomplishments as well as business accomplishments. Check out some of the name badges you see in retail establishments today. You will see badges like *"Serving you since xxxx"* I recently spoke at an event for New York Life agents that had been with the company less than two years. They celebrated the business milestones. You are probably asking yourself the question. What milestone could a new agent have? What about 6 months? 1 year? The number of new policies written? And the exuberance in the meeting when individuals were recognized was contagious. I only knew a couple of the agents, but I couldn't help but join in the applause as they recognized their peers.

Acknowledge a job well done. All of us like to be recognized for a job well done. Do you recognize your employees for a job well done? Do you have a most valuable employee program? The local hospital in town calls it the *Positive Posse*. Maybe it's just a small token that is handed out when a manager sees or hears that an employee has done something exceptional. Employees can collect these tokens and the tokens can be redeemed for a free lunch, a gift card, etc. You get the idea.

Many of the techniques used to create an attitude adjustment within your employees will also help develop fruitful employees. Developing fruitful employees will be discussed in detail in the *Fruitful Employee* chapter.

Thomas Jefferson said, *"Nothing can stop the man with the right mental attitude from achieving his goal; nothing on earth can help the man with the wrong mental attitude."*

Does your business have an attitude? Of course it does. Your business' attitude is a reflection of the attitude of each and every one of your employees. A business infected with the positive attitude contagion creates fruitful employees who feel respected and trusted, who enjoy a sense of belonging. A workplace infected with the positive attitude contagion increases engagement, which ultimately leads to improved productivity, improved moral and an improved bottom line.

Every day you can make a decision that will greatly impact your business. It is a decision about your attitude. How will you approach your business today? The choice is entirely yours.

"The longer I live, the more I realize the impact of attitude on life.

Attitude, to me, is more important than facts.

It is more important than the past, than education, than money, than circumstance, than failures, than successes, than what other people think or say or do. It is more important than appearances, giftedness, or skill. It will make or break a company, a church, a home.

The remarkable thing is we have a choice every day regarding the attitude we will embrace for that day. We cannot change our past ... we cannot change the fact that people will act a certain way. We cannot change the inevitable.

The only thing we can do is play on the one string we have, and that is our attitude.

I am convinced that life is 10% what happens to me and 90% how I react to it. And so it is with you, we are in charge of our Attitudes."

—Charles Swindoll

EVANGELICAL CHRISTIAN PASTOR, AUTHOR AND EDUCATOR

CHAPTER THREE

"Are we there yet?"

When Teresa and I first moved back to California from Connecticut, we lived in Bakersfield, California. Once every couple of months, either on the holidays or long weekends, we would pack the kids in the car and head to Grandma and Grandpa's house to visit. One of the reasons we moved back to California was so our children would get to spend some time with our parents. They lived in Santa Clara, California which was about a four-hour drive from Bakersfield. We would be on the road about an hour or so when from the backseat we would here, *"Are we there yet?"* and "How much longer Mommy?" The first few times we took the trip, the kids were not quite sure how long it would take. Once we took the trip a couple of times, they stopped asking until we were almost there. They had a mental time frame and a picture of where the landmarks, and the potty stops were in relation to their final destination. This leads me to ask a simple question. "Is it possible to get to where you're going without knowing where you're going?" You must be thinking to yourself, "What does he think I am, stupid?" The answer is of course not. You can't get to where you are going if you don't know where you're going. The same logic applies to both your personal life and your business. Without a clear mental picture of where you're going and what you're trying to accomplish, it's virtually impossible to achieve either.

Every individual and every business must absolutely know their desired future. It is your vision. I define vision as a vivid mental picture created by your imagination of what you're striving to achieve. Your vision is a critical element in the success of both you and your business. The clearer you are about your vision, the greater influence that clarity will have on what you are currently doing. With a clear vision you are much more capable of evaluating an activity in the present and determining whether that activity is consistent with where you truly want to be.

This may all seem very obvious but do you have a personal vision for yourself? I would venture to say that the majority of you reading this book do not have a personal vision let alone a vision for your business. Successful individuals, as well successful businesses, have a clear vision of where they are going. Your vision will take you and your business out beyond the present. It creates a mental picture of what you and your business is striving to become. A vision creates a vivid colorful picture that provokes emotion and excitement. It creates enthusiasm. It poses a challenge that inspires, engages people and builds commitment.

Creating Your Visions

A powerful vision should stretch your imagination. It should stretch your aspirations, and be created with an attitude of expectancy. I love this quote by George Bernard Shaw: *"You see things and ask 'Why?' But I dream things that never were and say' 'Why not?'"* Again your vision should stretch your imagination, stretch your aspirations, and be created with an attitude of expectancy.

This reminds me of the story of the pilot who came on the intercom midflight and said, *"I have some good news and I have some bad news. The bad news is we have lost all of our instrumentation and we do not know where we are. The good news is we have a strong tailwind and are making excellent time."* Is this an accurate picture of how you live? Many people have no direction for their life but they are sure getting their fast.

Take a moment now and reflect on your personal vision, your dream. Imagine that you are the full manifestation of your vision. You have magically appeared in your vision. Describe what you are experiencing and describe it as if it is happening right now. Your personal vision describes what you want to achieve in life. Your vision is about defining your purpose in life. Having trouble defining your vision? Just imagine you stopped at your neighborhood gas station to get gas on your way to work. You walk into the convenience store to get another cup of coffee and you notice a sign in the window. This week's lottery is $100 million. You usually don't buy a lottery ticket, but this time you purchase a single ticket. Next morning you open your morning newspaper and begin to check the numbers. The first number matches, and then the second, and the third, and the fourth, and your heart begins to race. You hit all the numbers. You just won the lottery. Your imagination runs wild. You begin to think of all the things you can do with the money—pay off the mortgage, buy a new car, take a vacation, start a college fund for the kids, and help your ailing parents. You create a mental picture of what you want to do in life. That's not your vision; those are your goals. People have a hard time differentiating between their vision and their life goals. Your vision is about your purpose in life, your why. It's not about your wants. I call your wants your Santa Clause list. Remember when you were a little kid and you wrote a letter to Santa with your wish list? You listed all the toys you wanted. To create your personal vision, reflect on the journey you're currently on and your life's purpose. Need a little help? The *Thinking Beyond the Obvious Success Action Guide* provides simple to answer questions that will stimulate your thinking and help you create your life's vision.

When you take your vision out of your imagination and put it on paper, clarity increases. Your vision needs to be accompanied by goals, goals that are **S**pecific, **M**easurable, **A**greed upon,

Relevant and with a Time commitment. The easy to remember acronym for establishing goals is S.M.A.R.T. When we focus on a target, a goal, a plan or a vision, we start to notice things that start to lead us there.

Remember this quote by Michelangelo when writing out your goals, *"The greatest danger for most of us is not that our aim is too high and we miss it, but that it is too low and we hit it."*

When writing out your goals consider each area of your life. Write out your goals with an expectancy that they will transpire. Consider your relationships, which include both family and friends. Consider your health, which includes not only your physical health but also your mental and spiritual health. Consider your business, and how you can be more engaged in what you are doing. Take into consideration your monetary situation and where you want to be financially. And lastly, ask yourself the question, *"What is the price I am willing to pay?"* Are you willing to give up watching television and spend the time learning a new skill? Are you willing to go back to school if that is what is required? Are you willing to go without something in order to save for something else? Are you willing to walk or exercise three–four times per week? Are you willing to improve your eating habits? In other words, are there changes you are willing to make in order to accomplish your goals?

Your personal vision is the cornerstone to your future success. Living life without a personal vision is living life aimlessly and without a direction. *Thinking Beyond the Obvious* is doing what most people don't. It starts with creating your own personal vision and goals.

In his book, *Awakening the Entrepreneur Within, How Ordinary People Can Create Extraordinary Companies*, Michael E. Gerber states, "A business without a vision has no soul; a business without a soul has no heart, no passion. A business without passion is a business whose demise has already been foretold."

Now take a moment and reflect on the vision for your business. Begin with the end in mind. Describe what your business looks like when it is exactly what you want it to be.

Create a mental picture of a healthy thriving business. You have been given free rein to stamp your identity on the business. Take the time necessary to create your vision for the business. Step by step guidance to creating your businesses vision can be found in the *Thinking Beyond the Obvious Success Action Guide*.

As you reread your vision, is there a powerful phrase that captures its essence and triggers a mental picture in the mind of everyone who reads it? If not, you will need to create one and this will be your vision statement.

Just think back to the 1980s when Microsoft first created its vision statement. It probably would have been considered by most to be highly unrealistic. The very simple statement, *"...a personal computer in every home running Microsoft software,"* doesn't seem so far fetched today. Or take the vision of Sergey Brin and Larry Page, co-founders of Google, when they walked into a venture capitalist's office seeking funding for their project.

Their vision for the company was contained in a simple, concise and memorable vision statement: *"Google provides access to the world's information in one click."*

And lastly, remember, Nike didn't say, *"We have the highest quality shoes made in the most state of the art processing facility in the world, made of the best materials available that are long lasting, durable and offered at an excellent price."* No, Nike said, *"Just do it."*

A vision statement creates commitment and understanding. It greatly improves the focus of the organization. A vision statement enables others who read it to understand how key individuals visualize the future. The clearer you are about your vision, the greater influence that clarity will have on what you are currently doing. Once again I cannot emphasize this enough. With a clear vision, you are much more capable of evaluating an activity in the present and determining whether the activity is consistent with where you truly want to be.

A vision statement not only describes the future position of the business but also creates commitment and understanding. It greatly improves focus and enables others who read it to understand how key individuals visualize the future of the organization.

In their book, *Full Steam Ahead! Unleash the Power of Vision in Your Company and Your Life*, Ken Blanchard and Jesse Stoner explain, *"It is important that all leaders in the company hold themselves and each other accountable for behaving consistently with the stated vision and values. As others see leadership living the vision, they will trust that leaders are serious and will be motivated to join."*

Creating a Shared vision

While your company's vision is extremely important, your employees will not buy into the business' vision if it is a top-down edict. Successful businesses have a shared vision. Is your own personal vision and the vision of your employees aligned with your company's vision? Is your company's vision aligned with your own personal vision and the vision of your employees? A shared vision is the creating of a business vision in which the direction of the organization satisfies both the individual goals of the employee and the business goals of the company. Employees must recognize that it is in their best interest to act in the company's best interest because the company's best interest considers the employee's best interest. If an employee recognizes that the company has their best interest in mind, that employee will exhibit a greater degree of commitment. A shared vision will foster commitment not just compliance.

A shared vision is a very powerful piece of communication. It paints a picture, which creates a desire, which builds a commitment. Organizations that do not allow others within the organization to have a hand in influencing their company vision are missing out on an opportunity to engage their employees. Employees will have a deeper understanding and commitment to a vision when they have a voice in creating the vision. A shared vision will blend the aspirations, career goals and personal vision of employees with the vision and goals of the organization. Step by step guidance on how to create a shared vision can be found in the *Thinking Beyond the Obvious Success Action Guide.*

To *Think Beyond the Obvious* is to align the company's vision with the employee's vision to create a shared vision. John F. Kennedy in his 1961 Inaugural Address challenged the American public to create a shared vision when he said, *"And so, my fellow Americans, ask not what your country can do for you—ask what you can do for your country. My fellow citizens of the world: Ask not what America will do for you, but ask what together we can do for the freedom of man."*

Two of the greatest challenges facing business leaders are, knowing how to bring your vision to life, and knowing how to how keep it going. It is the responsibility of leadership to ensure that people understand and embrace the vision of the organization. Bringing your vision to life requires engaging your employees in the process. Keeping your vision alive requires sharing the vision throughout the organization and continuously reinforcing your vision through your words and actions.

This quote by Wilbur Wright, of the famous Wright Brothers, in the early 1900's summarizes the importance of a shared vision. *"What one man can do himself directly is but little. If, however, he can stir up ten others to take up the task, he has accomplished much."* Have you stirred up ten others, fifty others or hundreds to take up your shared vision? Remember a shared vision is a powerful tool; it gives meaning to today and gives hope for tomorrow.

CHAPTER FOUR

"Me Too's" Fail

"**M**e Too's" fail, seem like pretty harsh words. Yes, "Me Too's" fail, no ands, ifs or buts about it. If you do not have a unique product with a unique message to a unique audience, you are a Me Too and destined for failure. Look around; you'll see countless examples of businesses that have closed, products that have failed, or soloprenuers that have struck out on their own only to find that maybe they were better off in an 8 to 5 job.

Stop and think for a moment. You are sitting at home one evening watching your favorite television program. You just viewed two TV commercials back to back. Most of the time you do not pay much attention to the commercials, but this time the commercials were for something that interested you, so you paid closer attention. Something was very unusual about the two commercials. They were for exactly the same products and the messages were exactly the same. Both were extolling the benefits of the product. The only difference was the product was manufactured by competing companies. You would have probably thought to yourself, "Boy that was ridiculous. Both companies were selling the same product and saying the same thing. What a waste of money." Sounds pretty ridiculous doesn't it?

Successful businesses, successful products and successful soloprenuers all have one thing in common. They all have a unique positioning. I define a unique positioning as *"a unique business, product, or service communicated via a unique message to a unique consumer."* We all know what it means to be unique. It means to be the only one of its kind. It means to be without an equivalent. A unique positioning is what differentiates a company's product or service from every other product or service in the marketplace. It answers the questions, *"Why should I do business with you or your company instead of a competitor? Why should I purchase your products?"*

Uniquely Positioning Your Business

Ever wonder why some businesses seem to prosper despite what is going on around them? They have the ability to win the devotion or following of a large number of people. They just seem to have a charisma about them. That charisma is their unique positioning. It is a differentiation that drives consumers to their business. It is a differentiation that drives consumers to purchase their products or solicit their services. It is a differentiation that allows their business to successfully compete in same competitive environment as each of their competitors. It is what makes your product or service more valuable to your customers and not just a *"Me Too."*

A unique positioning is the perception consumers have of your product or service. A unique positioning is not what you're telling your customers, but it's what your customers experience. It is what your customers are telling you. Your positioning must create a real or a perceived uniqueness. It must create points of differentiation in the minds of your customers. But, how many businesses do you see, how many soloprenuers do you know that are doing and saying exactly what every other business is saying or doing? *"Me Too"* businesses fail, *"Me Too"* products fail and a *"Me Too"* message is a waste of your valuable marketing dollars.

Your unique positioning should clearly establish in the minds of your consumers what you are known for. Imagine if you approached five of your best customers and asked them, "If you had to choose five words to describe my business, what would they be? What descriptive words would you use to describe my business?" Whether you like it or not, your business is described everyday by the words of others. Are your customers determining what those key words are or are you establishing those key words in the minds of your customers? You want the key words being created in the minds of your customers to be key words that you planted. Once those words are planted, those key words are reinforced by your actions; the experiences your customers have with the product or service.

Look at various businesses, what are they known for? What five words would you use to describe their business? Let's take McDonald's for example. The five words I would use to describe McDonald's are; fun, fast, consistent, kids, and value. Are your five words similar or different? McDonalds's, based on my experience with them, has created those words in my mind. McDonald's is fun with Ronald McDonald and the play areas in most of the stores. McDonald's is fast, you usually do not have to wait long for your order. McDonald's is consistent. Regardless what state and in some instances what country you are in, your McDonalds' hamburger and fries will taste pretty much the same. McDonald's is kids, the restaurants are kid friendly and the Happy Meal is targeted specifically at kids. And lastly, McDonald's connotes value in my mind with the addition of the value meals.

Your unique positioning when communicated to your unique customer must resonate with them. Your customers must feel after listening to your message that you are speaking directly to them. Do they say, *"That is exactly the service I need," or "that is exactly the product I need? How did you know?"*

Every Sunday with few exceptions, Teresa and I attend church. There are times during the pastor's sermon when I feel he is talking directly to me. Every point he makes is exactly what

I needed to hear. He is speaking directly to me. It's like he knows what's going on in my life and wrote the sermon specifically for me. And I don't doubt that it may have been the case some Sundays. Your communication message must be like the pastor's sermon, it must speak directly to each of your customers.

How you uniquely position your business can be done one of three ways. Each way has merit and is proven by a company's success. Once again, as I have done throughout the book, I am going to give you illustrations from my own experience or from what I have observed in businesses. This will help you create that intuitive understanding of the different types of positioning. Once you have that understanding, look at how you can uniquely position your business.

First you can create a positioning that is based on a rational connection between your product or service and your consumers. Secondly, you can create a positioning that is based on an emotional connection between your product or service and your consumers. The last way to position your business is by coupling the rational with the emotional to create an emotional but rational positioning.

Rational Positioning

A rational positioning is a unique positioning built around a product's attributes or benefits. It can be built around a product's price, quality or value proposition. It can also be built around a product's use or application. And lastly, it can be built around a product's competitor.

Baking soda is a product that has been around for more than 155 years. Church & Dwight, the makers of Arm & Hammer® Baking Soda, have used a rational connection approach to positioning Arm & Hammer® Baking Soda. Arm & Hammer® Baking Soda is positioned as pure, versatile, effective, environmentally safe, and economical. It can be used for baking and countless household and personal care uses. Dr. Austin Church and John Dwight formed the John Dwight & Co. to manufacture and sell sodium bicarbonate in the mid 1840's. Baking soda is made from soda ash and is mined in the form of an ore called trona.

Today Arm & Hammer® Baking Soda is positioned as a safe and effective cleaner, a deodorizer to be used in your refrigerator or down the garbage disposal. It can be used to deodorize carpets and pet beds. It can be used in baking. It helps make the dough rise. Arm & Hammer® Baking Soda can even be used in your pool to help maintain the pH of the water. It can help in the extinguishing of a small cooking fire. It is safe to use as an anti-acid to relieve heartburn, acid indigestion or a sour stomach when used as directed. By now you should get the picture of a product that is positioned based on product usage, a rational connection.

Federal Express is an example of a business that has also been built around a rational connection. Federal Express, *"When your package absolutely, positively has to get their overnight."* We all know the Federal Express story and if you don't it's worth repeating. In 1962 Fred Smith entered Yale University. While attending Yale he wrote a paper for an economics class. The paper detailed an overnight delivery service. Folklore suggests he received a C for this paper, although in a later interview he claims he told a reporter, *"I don't know what grade, probably my usual C,"* while other tales suggest that his professor told him that in order for him to get a C, the idea had to be feasible. The paper became the idea for Federal Express.

It is said that during an interview Smith said, *"The solution was in my mind to have an integrated air and ground system which had never been done before. By the early '70's when I had gotten out of the service it was very clear that a new society was coming in earnest. And so, at that point I said, 'What the hell, let's try to put it together.'"* And that is how FedEx came to be.

Emotional Positioning

An emotional positioning is creating a unique positioning built around a feeling such as love or hate toward your business, product, or service. Not sure hate would work. Creating an emotional connection is creating a psychological benefit. Satisfying a psychological need is understanding the consumer's lifestyle and how a product or service can help the consumer reach it.

Starbucks was built on a positioning that creates an emotional connection. The Starbucks experience has magnetism around it. Starbucks first store was opened in 1971 in Seattle's historic Pike Place Market. The name was derived from the book *Moby Dick*, written by Herman Melville. Starbucks began by providing coffee to fine restaurants and espresso bars. Howard Schultz, who had joined Starbucks as director of retail operations and marketing while on a trip through Italy, was impressed by the popularity of espresso bars in Milan. He had the idea to model a retail coffee business after the passion and style of the old world Italian coffee houses.

Schultz brought his idea to Jerry Baldwin, one of the original owners of Starbucks. Baldwin wasn't interested in selling cups of espresso, feeling it would detract from the original business, which was selling coffee beans. Howard Schultz, convinced that his idea was a big winner, left Starbucks to begin his own business. He called his new venture Il Giornale which was named after the largest daily newspaper in Italy.

In 1987 Schultz raised enough capitol to purchase Starbucks from Jerry Baldwin and Gordon Bowker. Schultz combined Starbucks and Il Giornale operations under the Starbucks brand. The experience of visiting a Starbucks was an intensely indulgent experience. There was the smell of fresh coffee, the indulgent flavored coffees, and the friendly baristas, who were not just servers. Starbucks created an emotional connection with its consumers. Although, there may be better coffees, the emotional positioning created by Starbucks has made it very difficult for a smaller independent coffee house to succeed.

Creating an emotional but rational positioning amounts to coupling the attribute driven or product benefit driven positioning with an emotional appeal. Gatorade is a good example of a product that started with a rational positioning that has evolved into a product with an emotional but rational positioning.

In the early summer of 1965, a University of Florida coach sat down with a team of doctors from the university. He asked them why so many of his athletes were being affected by heat and heat-related illnesses. The doctors discovered that two key factors were causing the problems. The fluids and electrolytes the players lost through sweat were not being replaced; neither were the large amounts of carbohydrates the players bodies used for energy. They formulated a carbohydrate-electrolyte beverage that replaces the lost components and called their concoction *"Gatorade."*

Gatorade is a product that was initially positioned rationally, but over the years an emotional positioning has been coupled with the rational positioning. Gatorade currently uses athletes in their commercials to extol its benefits. Gatorade creates an emotional connection with the consumer. In the case of Gatorade it is, *"I can be just like (insert athlete) if I drink Gatorade."*

Your positioning must fill a marketplace void, whether real or perceived, by the product or service you provide. It is the powerful perception (your positioning) your customers have of your business and the product or services provided that will drive business. *Think Beyond the Obvious* when creating your positioning. Your message needs to be so uniquely positioned that it speaks specifically to your prospects and customers.

Just like creating your vision statement was an important part of articulating your vision concisely. Your USP (Unique

Selling Proposition) is an important statement that helps you communicate your unique positioning.

Creating your Unique Selling Proposition

A *Unique Selling Proposition* (USP) is a marketing concept that was first proposed as a theory to explain a pattern among successful advertising campaigns of the early 1940's. Successful advertising campaigns made unique propositions to the customer that convinced them to switch or purchase the product. A USP is a distinct descriptive statement or concept that captures the essence of your positioning. It positively positions your business differently in the minds of the consumer.

An effective USP will breathe life into your business. Back in the 1960's, Avis the car rental company was struggling to compete with Hertz. It was a distant number two. Avis was struggling to create a *Unique Selling Proposition* or competitive advantage. So what did Avis do? Its advertising agency came up with an extremely powerful USP. *"We're number two. We try harder."* Avis still rented cars just like their competition, but it positioned itself as the company that worked harder, gave better service, and better rates. And all this was communicated through its USP. With it Avis made incredible progress towards establishing itself as a major player in the rental car business. Avis is now a major brand. Now what does an upstart company like Enterprise do? They create a USP that positions Enterprise as the company that will pick you up at your home or your place of work and bring you to the rental office. *"Pick Enterprise. We'll pick you up."*

Take two luxury car companies with unique positionings. Mercedes Benz positions itself as the car for those who want to drive a *"status symbol"* while BMW positions itself as the *"ultimate driving machine."* Both compete in the same market, but one is positioned to attract the consumer who is seeking the emotional connection to status while the other is positioned to attract those who want the emotional connection of the driving experience.

There have been a number of highly successful positioning statements over the years. How many of these you can identify?

1. *He keeps going and going and going*
2. *We bring good things to life*
3. *Can you hear me now?*
4. *Raising the bar*
5. *What's in your wallet?*
6. *Are you in good hands?*
7. *A diamond is forever*
8. *Every kiss begins with* _____
9. *It takes a licking and keeps on ticking*
10. *Betcha you can't eat just one*
11. *Is it soup yet?*
12. *M'm! M'm! Good!*
13. *Unleash the power of the sun*
14. *From the land of sky blue waters*
15. *Taste great, less filling*

16. *Good to the last drop*
17. *It's the real thing*
18. *Breakfast of champions*
19. *Mikey likes it*
20. *Snap, Crackle and Pop*
21. *The chocolate the melts in your mouth not in your hand*
22. *Think outside the bun*
23. *Where's the beef*
24. *You deserve a break today*
25. *I'd walk a mile for a _____*
26. *Leave the driving to us*
27. *See what brown can do for you*
28. *Fly the friendly skies*
29. *We really move our tails for you*
30. *Driver's wanted*
31. *Like a rock*
32. *Quality is job one*
33. *The ultimate driving machine*
34. *Zoom, Zoom, Zoom*
35. *Put a tiger in your tank*
36. *You can trust your car to the man that wears the star*
37. *You've got questions, we got answers*
38. *The few, the proud, the _____*
39. *Be all you can be*
40. *The toughest job you'll ever love*

1. Energizer Batteries
2. General Electric
3. Verizon Wireless
4. Cingular
5. Capitol One
6. Allstate
7. DeBeers
8. Kay Jewelers
9. Timex
10. Lays Potato Chips
11. Lipton Soup
12. Campbell Soups
13. Sunny Delight
14. Hamm's Beer
15. Miller Lite
16. Maxwell House
17. Coca Cola
18. Wheaties
19. Life Cereal
20. Kellogg's Rice Krispies
21. M & M's
22. Taco Bell
23. Wendy's
24. McDonald's
25. Camel Cigarettes
26. Greyhound Lines
27. UPS
28. United Airlines
29. Continental Airlines
30. Volkswagen
31. Chevrolet Trucks
32. Ford
33. BMW
34. Mazda
35. Esso/Exxon
36. Texaco
37. Radio Shack
38. Marines
39. Army
40. U.S. Peace Corps

Your USP must create a real or perceived advantage in the minds of your customer. It's a powerful statement that uniquely positions your company and differentiates you from other businesses.

The USP is also the beginning of building your brand. Your USP is not only what differentiates your business from your competitors, it becomes the essence of your brand. In a campaign developed in the early 1990's by Dow Jones, The Wall Street Journal issued the following statement regarding a brand: *"A brand or corporate image is not something that can be seen, touched, tasted, defined or measured. Intangible and abstract, it exists solely as an idea in the mind. Yet it is often a company's most precious asset … in a world of parity products and services nothing can tilt more things dramatically in your favor."*

Strong brands that are created through a strong USP enjoy distinct advantages. They are perceived as different from their competitors. They satisfy consumers' needs on both an intellectual and emotional level. And they consistently deliver on their brand promise.

Simply, your brand is the perception of your business or service that lives inside the mind of your customers. Your brand is the one thing that you want others to identify with. <u>A word of caution</u>. You must absolutely be able to deliver on the promise of your USP. After all, the future of your brand and how your business is perceived is dependent on it.

Small businesses that do not passionately weave their USP into the fabric of their business are taking an unnecessary risk. Your USP must be completely integrated into all aspects of your marketing. Every communication opportunity must speak with one voice.

Speaking with one voice is covered in detail in the chapter, *Marketing is Everything*.

CHAPTER FIVE

Marketing is Everything

L et's start with the fundamental principle of "what is marketing?" Marketing is one of the most misused concepts today. It is used interchangeably with advertising, but advertising is only a small part of marketing. This chapter is going to bring clarity to what marketing is for a small business. But let's first start with the traditional corporate America definition.

The American Marketing Association (AMA) defines marketing as follows: *"Marketing is an organizational function and a set of processes for creating, communicating, and delivering value to customers and for managing customer relationships in ways that benefit the organization and its stakeholders."*

Now I know why small business owners are confused and intimidated by marketing. I would avoid marketing too if I had to try to understand the AMA's definition. And I know what large corporate marketing is. After all, I spent 5 years working in a very traditional corporate marketing position in New York for a very large food company. A definition such as the one given by the AMA leads to avoidance, and avoidance does nothing to move your business ahead.

Marketing for a small business does not have to be as difficult or confusing as the corporate giants make it out to be. So what is the definition of marketing for a small business? I would say that marketing is every impression you or your business makes on a customer or a prospect.

Marketing is just not a department. Everyone in your company is a marketer. The receptionist whose voice may be the first sound your customers hear is marketing. The delivery person whose rear-end may be the last thing a customer sees is marketing. Every point of contact your business has with your customers is a critical part of marketing. As R. McKenna stated in his article in the Harvard Business Review, *"Marketing is not a function, it is a way of doing business … marketing has to be pervasive, a part of everyone's job description, from the receptionist to the board of directors."*

Every person in your organization plays an important role in marketing. Marketing is all the interaction a prospect or a customer ever has with your business. And I mean **all** interaction. We will call these interactions "consumer touch points." Consumer touch points include advertising, from the Yellow Pages to your website, to your television advertising, the ambience of your facility, the way in which your phone is answered, the way in which your customers are initially greeted, the cleanliness of your restrooms, and the appearance of your employees. The sum of all these experiences impacts and influences the impression your business makes on your customers.

Yes, even the cleanliness of your restrooms is important. Just recently, I was consulting with one of my clients who owns a sandwich shop. A middle-aged woman, who was professionally dressed, walked into the sandwich shop one day. She went straight to the women's restroom. My first thought was, she must really have to go. She peeked in the door and quickly walked back outside. I heard her say to the group of ladies she was with, "They're clean." The group of ladies came back in. They sat down and had lunch. Yes, marketing is everything.

Not to long ago I was working with a very successful eye surgeon. We were evaluating every aspect of his business. We looked at all the traditional elements of marketing. We looked at his collateral materials, i.e. brochures, as well as in-lobby signage, his website, his e-mail newsletter, his Yellow Page ad, and so on and so on.

As I was consulting with him one day, I said, *"OK Doc, this suggestion is going to be the least expensive marketing program you ever ran."* He looked at me and said, *"Robert, nothing you do is inexpensive."* My response was, *"This marketing idea is relatively inexpensive. I want you to go down to the local paint store and purchase a gallon or two of paint. I want you to paint your lobby and waiting room."*

You see the lobby and waiting room looked worn. They hadn't been refreshed in a while. While he did not go down to the paint store and buy a can of paint, he did have the lobby and the waiting room professionally painted.

How many of you can say you have looked at the interior of your restaurant, or the lobby of your waiting room, or the appearance of your store through the eyes of your consumers lately? I would venture to say that most of you have not. And when you do, you're looking with blinders on. You're not recognizing the impact and impression the interior, and for that matter, the exterior of your facility, will have on your consumers.

Back to the doctor's office. Once we refreshed the lobby and waiting room, we trashed all the old outdated magazines and subscribed to a number of new magazines. Now, while his patients are waiting, they can engage themselves in a new magazine. And we added Wi-Fi. I can hear you saying to yourself, "New magazines, Wi-Fi?" Answer this question, *"Wouldn't you want your waiting patients to be engaged in a magazine or checking e-mails instead of watching the clock and becoming frustrated and upset that you are a few minutes late?"*

This brings me to a story I once heard that reinforces the point that marketing is everything. A major airline CEO was walking through the aisles of a plane prior to the travelers boarding. He became extremely upset when he checked a couple of the tray tables and saw they were not clean. He called over the flight attendant and posed this question: *"If we can't keep something as simple as tray tables clean, do you think our customers will question whether we can keep an engine properly maintained?"*

Marketing is everything. Marketing is all interaction a customer or potential customer (prospect) has with your business. And it does not just apply to soloprenuers or businesses; it also applies to you personally. This is evident by a story William McKinley, the 25th U.S. President, once told. He had to choose between two equally qualified men for a key job. He puzzled over the choice until he remembered an incident that had previously happened. On a rainy night, McKinley had boarded a crowded streetcar. One of the men he was now considering had also been aboard, though he didn't see McKinley. Then an old woman carrying a basket of laundry struggled into the car, looking in vain for a seat. The candidate pretended not to see her and kept his seat. McKinley gave up his seat to help her. Remembering the experience which he called *"this little omission of kindness,"* McKinley decided against the man on the streetcar. Our decisions and our actions—even when they seem small and inconsequential tell a lot about us. (Story adapted from *Presidential Anecdotes,* Paul F. Boller Jr., Penguin, Books.)

Remember, marketing is everything. Marketing will influence what will be remembered about your business and the impression customers take away from your business. Marketing will influence what impression customers are leaving your business with. Marketing is the impression your employees are having on your customers. Marketing is the impression your office or store is having on your customers. Marketing is the impression your communication message is having on your customers and prospects.

Let me give you one more example of marketing that you may not think of as marketing at all, but which may help you develop that "*Thinking Beyond the Obvious*" mental picture that marketing is everything.

My brother-in-law Carl and I set out one beautiful morning to play a round of golf. We were at the first tee and I hit first. I hit my very typical first drive, not very long and not very straight. Carl was next. He took a couple of practice swings, and on the last one, the club head of his driver flew off. I noticed that the clubhouse pro had seen what happened but he did nothing. "Nothing" is what ordinary companies do. Carl proceeded to play the round of golf without his driver. At least it evened up the drives a little. He would only outdrive me by 25 yards, not the usual 50.

The clubhouse pro did not realize that marketing is everything. If he had, when he'd seen what happened, he would have walked over with a demo driver and let Carl take it for a test drive. In fact, as we made the turn between the 9th and 10th hole, he could have easily asked Carl if he would like to test-drive a different driver. You're probably saying to yourself, "But that is a $400 driver. What if he walks off with it?" A credit card or the car keys could have been easily left as a security deposit. Knowing Carl as I do, he would have purchased a new driver at the end of our round. He would have even paid a little more for both the convenience and the service provided. All the clubhouse pro had to realize was that marketing is everything.

Notice we hadn't even discussed advertising, but I gave you three examples of how marketing is everything. The clean restrooms in the sandwich shop and the clean trays on an airplane help develop a perception in the mind of the consumer, which begins to build the brand. The office décor creates an image in the mind of the patient, which begins to build a lasting impression. And don't forget the experience of William McKinley, who made a hiring decision based on an individual's actions. Or lastly, the clubhouse pro who missed an opportunity to sell a new driver.

Your Brand, The Lasting Impression

Your marketing builds and reinforces the lasting impression you want to leave in the minds of your customers. Successful marketing leverages and synchronizes every communication opportunity to build a lasting impression. Look down at your shoes for a moment. Is there a certain swoosh on them or do they have three stripes down the side? Or perhaps you are drinking a cup of coffee while you are reading this chapter. Is there a green circle on the cup? Or if you just returned from walking, does your drink bottle have a lightening bolt on it? What comes to mind when you think of golden arches? The little apple with a bite taken out of it? Or if you're a football fan, a blue/gray star with white trim? How about shopping at a store with a red and white bull's-eye? These are all examples of lasting impressions, the distinct identities, the collection of images and ideas that create the identities of products or companies. Successful companies do not just create products, they create brands that are distinctive. They create an identity that you quickly recognize.

Your brand is the sum of your customers' experiences at every interaction over the lifetime of the relationship. Your brand is built from the inside out and must be reflected through every interaction your business has with your customers. Your brand is what you promise reinforced by what you deliver. Your brand creates expectations in the minds of consumers. Consistently meeting the expectations of your consumers will reinforce your brand. Your brand defines who you are, how you operate, and what makes you different or unique. Small businesses can and must build their brand. Building your brand is a foundational cornerstone of your business. It is the essence of what your business is. Your business has to be built in such a way that it motivates the consumer to take immediate action. Most small business consultants will advise not to spend any money building your brand. They say that you can't afford it. They say leave building a brand to the corporate giants.

But, as a small business owner, you absolutely must maximize the efficiency and effectiveness of your marketing. In order to do that, you must couple brand building with direct response advertising.

I call this direct-response brand building. Direct-response brand building is the coupling of direct-response advertising with brand building image advertising. Direct-response brand building will build long-term equity in your business, and it will give you the immediacy of direct-response advertising.

Small businesses can and must build their business through direct-response brand building. As I indicated previously, small business consultants will advise you not to spend marketing dollars on building your brand. They will advise that all your marketing dollars must be spent on direct-response marketing only. They will advise that you do not have a marketing budget large enough, therefore all your advertising dollars need to be directed at direct-response only. Plainly and simply that is just ordinary thinking.

Provided below is an oversimplified illustration of two print advertisements you would possibly find in a Sunday newspaper insert or in a popular women's magazine. The first is a direct-response ad, and the second is a direct-response brand-building ad.

Although this is an overly simplified example for illustration purposes, the first ad only encourages the consumer to purchase the product and save $.50 on the soap indicated. It does nothing to reinforce and build the brand. The second ad, although very similar, is a direct-response brand-building ad. The ad still encourages the consumer to purchase the product and save $.50, but it also builds the brand by indicating the purchaser will get whiter clothes.

Over time the product will establish the brand, which will be known for whiter clothes. Direct-response in and of itself will not build the brand equity needed to differentiate your business from every other business in the marketplace. It is imperative that you couple direct-response with brand-building advertising. The two, when working together, will build a lasting impression. Strong brands are less likely to be viewed as a commodity. Strong brands develop a loyal following. Your customers become evangelists for your business. An evangelist is a customer who convinces others with zeal about the merits of your business. You know the type, When you ask for a restaurant recommendation, they are quick to let you know their favorite restaurant, their favorite dish, and even the waiter or waitress you should ask for. Don't we all wish that we had such evangelists for our businesses?

Building a brand establishes the impression your customers or prospects have of your business. It helps shape your business. The good will and equity you build by building a brand will lead your prospects and customers to view your business differently.

Expectations are established, and continually delivering or meeting those expectations will solidify your brand. The stronger your brand, the more difficult it is for your competitors to lure your customers away. Without a strong brand your business is no more than a commodity. Commodities are just a *"Me Too."* And as we have learned earlier *"Me Too's"* fail.

Integrated Marketing— Speaking With One Compelling Voice

Your marketing must be totally integrated. Integrated Marketing is synchronizing all marketing messages into one compelling voice. Integrated marketing is a communication strategy that considers how all the elements of your marketing communicate with the public. Businesses will spend billions of dollars marketing their products and services. Consumers are exposed to a great variety of messages from a vast array of sources everyday. These sources include advertising, sales promotion, public relations, internet advertising, e-marketing, causal and event marketing, collateral materials, i.e., sales brochures and business cards plus telephone marketing, trade shows, sponsorships, or viral marketing.

Today's consumer moves in and out of these multiple marketing mediums without a second thought, consequently, businesses must ensure communication is seamless, relevant, and consistent across every consumer touch point. There is no excuse for consumer interaction with your business being disjointed or inconsistent. All too often businesses fail to integrate their various communications into one compelling voice. Conflicting messages from various marketing channels can result in a confused consumer and a confused consumer will not be an evangelist for your business.

The American Association of Advertising Agencies defines Integrated Marketing as the "concept of marketing communication planning that recognizes the added value of a comprehensive plan that evaluates the strategic role of a variety of communication disciplines (general advertising, direct response, sales promotion, and public relations) and combines these disciplines to provide clarity, consistency, and maximum communication impact." That's hogwash, simply said, Integrated marketing helps businesses connect with their customers and prospects by synchronizing all marketing messages into one compelling voice.

Are all the elements of your marketing working together? Is your marketing message consistent across all customer touch points? Will a visitor to your business have the same impression of your business as the customer who calls your business or visits your website? Does your advertising communicate the same message as your sales brochure or your public relations campaign?

Successful marketing synchronizes every communication opportunity. Whether the message is an internal message or an external message, a non-verbal message or a verbal message, each element must be synchronized with the other. All too often companies fail to integrate their various communications. Mass advertising says one thing while the company sales brochures say something else, and their website says something altogether different. Many times that is the result of different people or agencies working on the business without understanding the overall marketing strategy.

Marketing was established earlier as every impression you make on a customer or a prospect. Integrated marketing is a consistent message across every consumer touch point. Marketing is becoming more and more challenging and less and less effective. As a result it is much more difficult to reach the consumer who is being bombarded by messages everywhere they turn. Today's messages must be totally integrated to improve efficiency and maximize the return on your investment. Consumers are demanding relevancy and consistency across all marketing communication channels. There is no excuse for a dialogue with a customer to be disjointed or irrelevant. In other words, every communication message must be consistent with the image you are trying to convey or the brand you are trying to build.

Every aspect of the customer's experience has an impact on the business, whether it's positive or negative. The value and strength of a business is the sum total of all the customers' experiences created at every touch point. Integrated Marketing should be viewed as if you are reading a book. Each chapter builds the characters and the plot. If you leave a chapter out the story becomes disjointed and the reader more than likely will not continue with the book. Each chapter contributes towards the book. Your marketing should be viewed the same way. Each element must contribute toward the brand, just like each chapter contributes towards the book. The idea of Integrated Marketing is not new. Walt Disney was using what he called *"synergy"* in the 1950's and 1960's to drive the Disney Company forward. Disney used a coordinated marketing effort between print, television, movies, merchandising, and the theme parks. Each part of the Disney marketing mix reinforced the other aspects of the mix that when viewed together built the Disney brand of today.

It has been said, and I truly believe that the whole of a marketing campaign can be greater than the sum of its parts, if those parts work tightly together to assist one another.

CHAPTER SIX

Is It "Mommy Clean"?

As Teresa and I were raising our children, they, like most children, had chores they had to do. Some chores were daily, like setting the table or cleaning the table after dinner. Other chores were weekly. One of the weekly chores was that they had to clean their rooms.

During the week, we would just shut the doors to their rooms. Early on we tried to coax them to clean their rooms on a daily basis. But, no matter how hard we tried, it was a battle we kept losing. It was a battle that was not worth fighting, given the fact that there were bigger battles to fight, battles like getting all their homework done. Finally we came to an agreement with them that they would be responsible for straightening their rooms every Saturday morning. Straightening meant picking-up all of the toys, putting all the dirty clothes in the dirty clothes basket, organizing their books and electronic games, dusting the furniture and lastly, vacuuming the carpet. They couldn't go out and play with their friends until their rooms were clean.

When they thought they were done cleaning, they would say, "Mom, I'm done," as they headed out the door. Teresa would stop them in their tracks and lead them back into their rooms for inspection. If the rooms were not completely clean, or if things were not put back in their places, they would have to finish the job. As the kids become older, Teresa would no longer have to take them back into their rooms. She would simply ask, *"Is it mommy clean?"* In other words, was it executed with excellence?

The late Martin Luther King, Jr. said it this way: *"If a man is called to be a street sweeper, he should sweep streets even as Michelangelo painted or Beethoven composed music or Shakespeare wrote poetry. He should sweep streets so well that all the hosts of heaven and earth will pause to say, 'Here lived a great street sweeper who did his job well.'"*

Can you truly say that everything you do in your business is done well, with excellence? Executing well and with excellence is making sure it is, *"Mommy clean"*.

This would include marketing, sales, customer relations, vendor relations, purchasing, manufacturing, inventory control, shipping and receiving, order entry and fulfillment, invoicing, customer support and accounts receivable and payable. You get the picture. It includes everything, and hopefully, I did not leave anything out. If I did, it belongs on the list.

This brings me to a story about my mom. My mom, bless her heart, is 90 years old and still volunteers at the information desk of the local Kaiser Hospital. One day I was in town for a business meeting and I decided to stop by the hospital and say hello to my mom. As I approached the information desk, I noticed that she had a line waiting for her. What was unusual was that there were other volunteers who were not assisting people. When she was done with her shift, we walked out together and I asked her, *"Mom, why do you think everyone comes to your station?"* Her response was quite simple: *"I just treat them like I would want to be treated."*

Most of the time, she was providing directions to doctors' offices, x-ray lab, or the pharmacy. Most of the people who used the information desk were either elderly or were a member of a minority. The hospital policy was to show them a map with the "You are here" arrow and point on the map where they need to go. My mom doesn't exactly follow protocol, but after 30-plus years of volunteering, who are they to question what she does? My mom will get out from behind the desk and give very specific directions. She will indicate the landmarks along the way. Sometimes she will walk down the hall with people, making sure they are clear about where they are going. After all, that is what she would expect a volunteer to do for her.

Everything done in your business which converts a product or service into a profit needs to be done well and with excellence.

It needs to be *"Mommy clean".* Although I listed a number of the executional elements, we will only discuss three of the processes here. Once again, my purpose is to help you create a mental picture and an intuitive understanding of what it means to execute with excellence, to help you answer the question, *"Is it Mommy clean"?*

Your Customer Experience

You would think that all businesses would realize that a great customer experience is critical to the success of business. But you would be surprised how many businesses are not meeting the expectations of their customers. In today's competitive global marketplace, a consistently excellent customer experience distinguishes the winners from the losers. People are searching—literally searching—for businesses that will treat them the way they want to be treated. Remember the golden rule our parents would teach us: Do unto others as you would have them do unto you? Are you treating your customers the way you would like to be treated? Can you say you are implementing the golden rule in your business? Today's consumers expect more than just low prices or a good product. They expect to be treated well and nothing less.

Several studies have indicated that 68% of consumers have stopped doing business with a business because of a bad experience or how they were treated and made to feel. Twenty percent of those consumers will never do business with the company again.

You cannot afford to bring customers in the front door only to lose them out the back door due to a poor customer experience. By leaving out the back door, your customer may go quietly and unnoticed, but not all of them will.

Social media today makes it extremely easy for a customer to blog a comment or tweet it to their contacts. You can easily search the internet and find disgruntled customers posting negative comments about an experience with a business they might have had. Research a product and you will find countless comments on whether the product is liked or disliked. It's like having your own consumer report available at your fingertips. Have you ever thought you wanted to purchase a particular product only to have your mind changed due to the number of negative postings you discovered while researching the product on the internet?

Recently Teresa and I were in the market to purchase a new HD television. We needed to replace our older 50" big box TV. I was responsible for determining whether we should purchase an LED, LCD or Plasma and which make and model. It was enough to make my head spin. The first place I visited was a well-known electronics store.

I was standing in front of the massive display of TVs and I called over the sales associate to ask her the simple question, "What is the difference between LED, LCD and Plasma?" Her answer was, "It's just a matter of personal preference." I was floored. I had already researched the differences and I knew it went beyond personal preference. I was just looking for confirmation of what I had already researched. I looked at her and said, "Thank you very much," and left the store.

My next stop was a major retailer who carried the same brands as the electronics store. I asked the same question of the sales associate. His answer was completely different. He proceeded to explain the differences and also asked me a few questions about my viewing habits, including, "Will you be using the TV for gaming?" and "Do you watch action movies?" and "Do you watch a lot of sports?" After I answered, he advised me what TV benefits best suited my viewing habits. Teresa and I returned to the store later that evening and asked for the sales associate who had been so helpful earlier in the day. Once again he walked Teresa through what he had explained to me earlier in the day. We purchased the TV that night. It was delivered two days later and we are extremely happy with our decision.

Based on my research prior to visiting the store, I had already pretty much made up my mind which type of TV I was going to purchase. My objective, by asking the sales associate to clarify the differences, was to confirm and reinforce my decision. Most times consumers experience what is called cognitive dissonance after they make a major decision. Cognitive dissonance is an uncomfortable feeling caused by holding two contradictory ideas simultaneously such as, "I made the purchase but did I make the right purchase?" After making a large purchase, consumers will usually seek positive information about the purchase to justify their decision. My asking the question of the sales associate was my attempt to justify the decision I was about to make and minimize post-purchase cognitive dissonance.

Lesson here: the reputation of any business can be affected by just one person. In the case of the first store that person happened to be the first sales associate who told me the only difference between the TVs was "personal preference."

The key point here is, if you are executing with excellence and consistently providing a positive customer experience, you will retain and win the loyalty of your customers, even with the number of competitive choices available. Satisfied customers become loyal customers. Are your customers satisfied? In our increasingly competitive business environment, a customer's loyalty is critical to a business' success. Once you get people in the door, you need to give them a reason to keep coming back. A positive customer experience is one way to keep people coming back. It's like making a deposit in your customer experience bank account. The negative experience is like making a withdrawal and the negative experience drains the account much quicker than a positive experience fills it.

In the example of my purchasing the TV, lucky for them I only walked out and did not post a complaint on one of the many consumer complaint sights. I did not go to the electronic retailers' website and post a negative comment about my experience, although a number of consumers would have done just that. Will I go back to the large electronics store if I need electronic equipment? Right now I am not quite sure; I have not had enough positive experiences or deposits in my customer experience bank account to offset that one negative experience. Remember the reputation of any business can be affected by just one person.

Successful businesses recognize the importance of the customer experience. They design every aspect of the company with the customer in mind. Everyone within the organization is a champion for the customer. So ask yourself this one important question about your business. *"Are you making a positive customer experience deposit with each customer transaction?"*

Everyone is a Critic

Today, each and every customer is a critic. With camera phones and instant messaging, a customer experience, whether positive or negative, can be instantly posted on the web through things such as You Tube, blogs or Facebook. If you owned a restaurant and the local newspaper food critic was in your restaurant and you knew who they were, wouldn't you do everything you could to make their experience memorable? Remember, in this highly competitive environment and with the advent of technology, everyone is a critic. Your business is under continuous surveillance, just like in the detective movies, where they hide across the street and take pictures of every one who enters or leaves the building. The detective in this case is your customer. Most everyone today carries a camera and in a number of instances, a video camera. It just happens to be their phone.

I can't help but recall a video that was taken early one morning prior to the opening of a fast food restaurant. Mice were scurrying about, and the video was posted on U-Tube before the store even opened. Since everyone is a critic, what steps would you take if you knew that the service you are providing or lack of it would be shared immediately? Would you change the way you operate or the way you service your customers or clients?

Here is another example of how we are all critics. Teresa had always wanted to visit Ireland, so to celebrate our 35th anniversary, we spent two weeks staying in bed & breakfasts and touring Southern Ireland. One evening, we decided to have dinner at the Hard Rock Café in Dublin. We had eaten at a number of Hard Rock Cafés throughout the world and thought we would add the Dublin Eatery to our list, although we had a variety of choices in the Temple Bar District of Dublin. As we entered the restaurant, we were greeted by a hostess and led to a table. We sat at the table for at least 15 minutes without a server stopping by to ask for our beverage or dinner order. A number of servers were in the area, and even with my giving them the "we are ready" sign, they did not stop at the table.

So what did we do? We walked out and had dinner at a small Irish pub. When we returned home, I did something I normally do not do. I posted a comment about our lack of service on a Dublin Ireland Restaurant review page.

On the other hand, the pub we ended up eating at was very attentive to our needs. They quickly seated us and a server immediately asked us what we would like to drink. And of course, I had the Irish standard, a pint of Guinness. The food was very good and we ended up eating at this particular pub a second time. During our Ireland trip we ate at a number of Irish pubs. They had a bar fare menu that was much less expensive than eating at a restaurant. The Irish pubs would be similar to eating at a casual dinning restaurant such as Chili's or an Applebee's.

From that one experience at the Hard Rock Café, I now have a different attitude towards all Hard Rock Café's. I now ask myself, "What business are they in? Are they in the restaurant business or are they in the business of selling Hard Rock Café merchandise?" I now believe it is the latter.

What can a business owner learn from this experience? Businesses need to strive for excellence each and every day. Your business and your brand are only as strong as the most recent impression a customer or prospect has because everyone is a critic. What steps would you take if you knew that the caliber of service you provided would be shared immediately? Would you change the way you operate? Would you change the way you service your customers? I hope so. I hope that by now you recognize you must make sure it is *"Mommy clean"*. You may not get a second chance.

Operations

Businesses must reinvent their business continuously. They must become their own competition before others do. How do you become your own competition? You continuously look for ways to improve all aspects of the business. You look for solutions that are outside the boundaries of ordinary thinking in everything you do. Previously, in chapter one, I discussed what Sherwin Williams had done to improve the paint can. That example could have easily been used here to illustrate the need to be your own competition.

In my position as president, although plant operations was not my area of expertise, I can remember continuously challenging the VP of Operations. I would always ask what I thought was a simple one-word question: "Why." And if I thought we didn't drill down far enough, I would ask the question again. At times he probably thought I was worse than a small child who was always asking, "But why?" Today in your operations, whether it is a restaurant, a processing plant, or a retail establishment, you must continuously look for ways to improve what is being done. You must look for ways to be more efficient. You must continuously drill down and ask, "Why?" or "Why not?" You must look for ways to reduce waste. There was a "Hells Kitchen" TV episode where the star of the show, the fiery chef, had the restaurant owner and the staff rummage through the dumpster and separate all of the food that was wasted that day. It added up to hundreds of dollars of product—a significant amount of waste that was not generating any income. As the restaurant owner was knee high in garbage, I bet he got the message.

Continuous Improvement

There is a philosophy that I believe we have lost sight of that was developed by the Japanese post World War II called "Kaizen." Kaizen is the Japanese word for "improvement." It refers to a practice that focuses on making continuous improvements in a business. Kaizen involves setting standards, reviewing progress toward meeting those standards and continuously setting those standards higher.

When I worked as an executive in the dried fruit business, we explored how we could become a worldwide entity. A strategic decision was made to expand the current product offering to include bulk raisins. Our target was to sell bulk raisins to the food and candy processors in both the United Kingdom and Japan. The companies targeted were Cadbury, Mars, and Shoei Foods. These companies had extremely tight specifications for the raisin products they purchased. They would only allow a limited number of capstems per 30 lb. box. A capstem is a little stem that held the raisin to the vine. These would usually be removed through the initial process, but a few capstems always remained. In order to break into this new arena, we needed to find a way to efficiently and effectively sort out the remaining raisins that had capstems. A capital investment was made, and an Elbascan laser was purchased and installed. The Elbascan laser was initially used in the almond industry and was now being adapted to sort raisins. The Elbascan would detect both foreign objects, such as rocks, and the raisins that had capstems. The scanner would send a message to the computer and the rock or capstem would be removed by a short burst of air.

Entering this new area of business for the plant also meant a complete shift in thinking by everyone working on the production side. The plant previously only packaged items sold in grocery stores. The specifications for grocery retail items were not as stringent as the specifications for the new channel of business the plant was entering. Each of these targeted companies that purchased high specification bulk product would send personnel to inspect the plant. They would review and evaluate every aspect of the business to determine whether the plant qualified as an approved vendor. Upon completion of their evaluation, the inspectors would sit with management personnel and review their findings.

Kaizen is a process that involves everyone in the plant, from the equipment operators to the plant manager, working together to improve the process. Basically, every aspect of your operations is analyzed and anything that creates waste is eliminated. And that is not just product waste. Waste is defined as anything that does not add value. It could be product waste, unnecessary inventory levels, time delays or the excessive handling of product. Monitoring and controlling inventory levels are where the term J.I.T (Just In Time) originated. J.I.T. reduces inventory carrying costs by minimizing the amount of inventory on hand. But it must be accomplished without compromising the service level. Any operation can benefit from Kaizen as long as there is a commitment to discard conventional fixed ideas and think beyond the obvious. Striving for operational excellence within your business is a must. It must become part of the business culture. It is must be the responsibility of everyone.

Marketing

As the business landscape has changed, marketing is now the responsibility of everyone in the organization. It no longer involves just the marketing manager or the product manager or whatever title corporate America gives the person responsible for the company's marketing efforts. In fact, companies have now created the senior executive officer title of Chief Marketing Officer (CMO). The marketing authority may belong to the CMO but the responsibility belongs with every employee in the organization. Businesses must look for ways to continuously connect with their consumers and it takes everyone within the organization to accomplish this key task. Chapter 5, *Marketing Is Everything*, covers in detail the critical role marketing plays in a business.

CHAPTER SEVEN

"Fruitful Employees"

We have continuously heard others tell us that employees are the lifeblood of an organization. But, are they really? Is the unmotivated, uninspired, only in it to-make-a- buck employee, the lifeblood of your organization? Is the employee that is sleepwalking through their day the lifeblood of your business? Is the employee that is stealing from the till the lifeblood of your organization? If he or she is, you have a serious problem.

No, *"Fruitful Employees"* are the lifeblood of your business. A *"Fruitful Employee"* is an employee that is not just doing their job and doing it well; a Fruitful employee has the best interests of the company in mind. They are engaged. They feel a connection to the company. They take pride in what they do. They do it with an energetic passion.

When employees have a sense of purpose to their jobs that goes beyond earning a paycheck, they are engaged, and engaged employees are *Fruitful Employees. Fruitful Employees* will find ways to work more efficiently. They will find ways to work smarter.

Studies tell us that 80% of working employees are not passionate about what they're doing. What that means is that four out of every five people you meet will not be happy in their job: they will not feel satisfaction, they are unfulfilled and uninspired. These employees are not *Fruitful Employees*.

In discussions with the employees of my clients, I usually ask them the following question: "What are some of your biggest complaints?" One of the complaints that surfaced most often was they did not feel that they were sufficiently recognized by their employer for the work they did. I would hear comments like, "My boss doesn't appreciate me," or "The owner of the company doesn't even know I exist," or "They don't know what I do for them."

If your employees do not feel appreciated, recognized, or respected they will not be *Fruitful Employees*.

Fruitful Employees can have a dramatic effect on your business. A positive attitude as well as a negative attitude can extend to your customers, suppliers, or other employees. Think about the last time you had a rude or grumpy waiter or waitress in a restaurant. Did that person's attitude have an effect on you?

When I owned the sandwich shops, I would always tell my employees that they could check their grumpy, negative attitude at the door when they arrived at work. If they had to, they could pick it back up when they left. Whether you are eating at a fine dining establishment, a casual dining restaurant, or the local sandwich shop, the attitude of the employees can dramatically affect the experience of the customers. It has even been noted that the attitude of a waitress or waiter can set the tone for a business luncheon. A rude and grumpy employee can have an impact on the results of the lunch.

Like the grumpy waiter at a restaurant, a rude, grumpy owner, executive, or manager can dramatically impact everyone around them. The receptionist in your office, who is normally friendly and cheerful, is now affected by your grumpiness and rudeness. She is no longer a cheerful, friendly person and it is reflected in her conversation with a major customer. Do you believe your receptionist can have a major impact on your business? Of course she or he can.

Successful businesses recognize that they need *Fruitful Employees*. They will look for ways to hire and develop these employees. After all, a product can be copied, and technology can be duplicated, but it is extremely difficult to replicate the passion and commitment of a *Fruitful Employee*.

Management must lead the way

The first step to creating fruitful employees is that management must lead the way. Whether you are the owner, part of the executive staff, or a manager you must lead the way. You must lead the way by your attitude, words, and actions. Your behavior needs to reflect the behavior you expect from your employees.

Consider, for instance, the statement from the ancient book, *Tao Te Ching*, written by the Chinese philosopher, Lao-tzu:

"But as for the best leaders, the people hardly notice their existence, the next best the people honor and praise, the next the people fear, the next the people hate. But when the best leader's work is done, the people say, 'We did it ourselves.'"

I can remember back to a time when as a senior executive of a mid-size company, I had to lead the way. A small company, based in the United Kingdom, purchased the dried fruit division of a major food company. It was a way to expand their holdings and enter the U.S. market. The new owners hired an entirely new executive team, of which I was a part, to manage the newly purchased company. The company did, however, retain the senior and middle managers, as well as the staff employees. So here was the dilemma—long-time managers and employees, some pretty set in their ways, now reported to a new executive team. The question that we deliberated on for days was, *"How do we build a cohesive team, and how do we re-engage the existing employees?"*

We decided that in order to re-engage the employees, we would hire an outside consulting firm to conduct a motivational, team-building event. The event took place in the beautiful mountains just below the entrance to Yosemite National Park and lasted two days.

The first event of the first day was to climb a pole about as high as a telephone pole and to jump off. In fact, as I recall, it may have even been a telephone pole. Of course, we were fitted with a harness that was connected by a rope to a pulley that was above the pole. The participants on the ground held on to the rope to keep us from falling. The rope was also used to lower those who could not make it to the top and wanted to come down. But, this was not on option for me because of my leadership position. The facilitator asked for the first volunteer. As I looked around, nobody was stepping up, I volunteered to go first. Part of me was saying, "Robert you're a company executive. Just stand back and watch the day's proceeding from the sidelines." Isn't that what a lot of senior executives or business owners do? They sit back and watch from the sidelines. But, I knew if I wanted these employees to follow us into corporate battle, I was going to have to go first. And believe me, I was scared out of my wits.

Step by step I climbed the spikes that protruded from the sides of the pole. I climbed and I climbed, trying not to look down, but focusing straight ahead at the pole. My legs were trembling as I climbed towards the top. As I got to the top, I realized that making the climb was the easiest part. The hard part was yet to come. I had to somehow stand on the top of the pole and the standing space was about the size of a dinner plate. It had just enough room for me to get both feet on.

Now, I didn't have the spikes to hold on to. I had to step on the top of the pole and push up with one foot while balancing myself. I managed to stand on the top of the pole and look around. The pole seemed as if it was swaying about ten feet from side to side, but it was probably not swaying at all, or maybe just a little. It was a beautiful, clear sunny day with not even a breeze. Next I had to jump off. I took a glance downward and saw the office staff cheering me on. Only half of them were there that first week due to the fact that business must go on. The rest of them would participate in the exercises the next week. Yes, I would have to climb the pole and jump again.

There was a bell hanging about five feet out from the top of the pole. We were to jump out toward the bell and on our way down ring it. I jumped out and did manage to ring the bell. I felt like I was in a free fall for several seconds. Then the rope harness caught me. I was lowered to the ground to a group of cheering, high-fiving employees. Due to my leading the way in that first event, the staff all participated. Not everyone made it to the top. Some climbed halfway and then climbed back down. Others made it to the top and could not stand on the dinner-sized plate standing place. They were lowered to the ground by the rope harness, but everyone encouraged everyone else. The ice was broken and a new company culture was beginning to be established. Those two days provided a positive bonding experience between the new management team and the staff of old. We were now becoming one cohesive team.

I recognized right then and there the importance of management leading the way. Sitting on the sidelines and giving direction was not an option. The same can be said about how you run your own business or manage your own staff. Sitting on the sidelines giving directions is not an option. In order to develop fruitful employees, management must lead the way.

A couple of years after the pole-climbing event, I was appointed president of that same company. One of my first objectives as president was to improve communication between the union employees and management. I wanted to make absolutely sure that the employees felt comfortable talking with me in my new position as president. Each day I would join them in the lunchroom, I would sit down at a lunch table and try to engage in their conversations. I was hoping they would realize that I truly wanted to participate in their conversations. I would sit at a different table every day but each time I sat at a table there'd be an eerie silence. The employees would begin excusing themselves, indicating that they needed to get back to work. I wasn't having much luck, and I was extremely frustrated.

Not only would I join them in the lunchroom, I would walk around the production facility by myself. I would walk around without the vice-president of operations or the department managers. (The old MBWA, Management By Wandering Around, principle) I would talk with the employees on the various productions lines. I would even try to talk to them in my broken Spanish, which was the native language for most of them. But, I just couldn't seem to earn their trust. I still was not getting the open dialogue of communication that I wanted.

Finally, I remembered reading in a business book about a manager who was also having a problem getting the employees to share with him their concerns. The employees were probably afraid of retribution. He proceeded to give the management team a stack of Monopoly, "Get Out of Jail Free" cards. Taking from what I had read, I printed a stack of Get Out of Jail Free cards and gave some to each of the managers with the following instructions: "Hand these to all the employees and explain the purpose of the cards." The cards could be given to any member of the management team, including myself. The employee that received the card could meet with any of the managers to discuss whatever issue he or she had with no recourse or retribution. Initially, the employees were reluctant to use the cards. But as word spread that management was truly listening, more and more employees began to meet with management including me. There were countless times when employees would venture upstairs during their break with their Get Out of Jail Free card in their hand. They would walk right past my administrative assistant and straight to my desk, where they'd share their concerns and ideas. I would always let them know what follow-up steps I would take. And of course, I would give them a new Get Out of Jail Free card. Once the employees realized that management was concerned and had their best interest in mind, they began to share openly. This was a *Thinking Beyond the Obvious* solution to opening the lines of communication between union employees and management. Now, when I would go into the lunchroom to sit with employees during their breaks, a number of employees would yell, "*Jefe, sientase aqui*," which means "boss sit over here."

Truly listen to your employees

Employees will be much more fruitful when they believe that their ideas will be heard. But squandered or untapped ideas are a major source of employee discouragement, frustration, and disengagement.

Let me relate a story of what happened recently to my oldest son Matthew. Matthew was working for a small family-owned business. And I mean a family business—a business where the dad, the mom, their daughter, two of their sons and son in-law all worked. Matthew's responsibility was to assemble electronic components that were part of a larger unit.

Ever since he was a little boy, Matthew had loved to put things together. We still have a large plastic container full of his Lego's. Matthew has the innate ability to see things a little differently. When he played with his Lego's he would initially follow the instructions and build the model. But, then he would try to figure out different ways to make things using the same Lego's.

For months, he was constructing these components for the company's units, his mind would try to figure out an improved way of doing it. One day he called me, "Dad, he said, "Can I come and visit? I want to talk to you about an idea I have." Sure Matt, I said. "Why don't we meet for lunch?"

I do not know a young bachelor living on a fixed income who is going to turn away a free meal. I met him for lunch the next day, and he shared with me how he had an idea that would reduce the amount of materials used in the unit and possibly save the company money. I advised Matthew to take it to his immediate supervisor and he did. But it fell on deaf ears. You see, this was a family business and ran like a family business. His immediate supervisor was not a member of the family and didn't want to do anything to rock the boat. He didn't want to take the idea to the owner of the company.

Well, Matthew called again and said. "Dad, what should I do? I really believe this idea will work, but my supervisor wouldn't even listen to it." In my consultant's role, I asked Matthew, "What do you think you could do?" His response was, "Next time the owner is in the shop and he asks how I'm doing, I am going to share my idea with him. It could save the company money." I said, "Great idea, Matthew."

So next time the owner was in the facility, Matthew did exactly what he said he was going to do. He was just starting to share his idea with the owner when the owner abruptly interrupted him and said, "Matthew we are not going to change the way we are doing things. Just do your job." The owner didn't even hear Matthew out.

As I indicated earlier in this chapter, untapped ideas or squandered ideas are a major source of employee frustration and lead to employee disengagement. How do you think Matthew felt when he called to share his experience? He was extremely frustrated. He said, "Dad, I can't believe he didn't even listen. That's not the way you should run a business." Matthews's comments were very insightful for a young adult with no formal business training. Maybe he was truly listening to some of the dinnertime conversations Teresa and I would have. After that, he became completely disengaged and is no longer working for the company.

Could the owner have approached Matthew differently that would have kept Matthew engaged? Whether the idea was a good one or not, is not the issue. The issue is employee engagement. It is simply listening to the idea. Maybe indicating he would look at it, or even test it in a unit to verify if it would work. This would have gone a long way in keeping Matthew engaged. Who knows maybe the idea could have saved the company some money.

Let's compare my son's experience to what recently occurred at The Martin Guitar Company. The Martin Guitar Company's story began in 1796 in Marknewkirchen, Germany with the birth of Christian Frederick Martin Sr. He was born into a cabinet making family and took up cabinet making at an early age. At the age of 15, he left his hometown and travelled to Vienna, Austria to apprentice under Johann Stauffer a renowned guitar maker. He immigrated to the United States arriving in New York in 1833 and started Martin Guitar.

CF Martin V1, at the age of 30, took over the family business when he was appointed Chairman and CEO. The business was struggling as he indicated in an interview. "Business was actually very difficult at that time." So what did Martin do? He thought beyond the obvious and did what others before him did not. He changed the culture. He did away with the traditional organizational chart system of management and engaged the employees. He encouraged employees to suggest ways to improve efficiency while maintaining product quality. I love this quote by Martin, *"You need to tap into the genius of the person doing the work,"* Today the business is about four times bigger than when he took over. It's no longer a little family run business, but a worldwide operation.

Quite a contrast from the experience my son Matthew had when he tried to make a suggestion on how a process might be improved.

This reminds me of one last example of truly listening to your employees. I was attending a training workshop on TQM (Total Quality Management) a number of years ago. The training was conducted by Phillip Crosby, a protégé of Dr. Edwards Deming, who created the 14 points for management. He also was world renowned for helping businesses as well as for teaching the Japanese business principles after the Second World War. Crosby related a story of an early TQM meeting at United Airlines which included both management and union employees. One of the union employees suggested that United make the head of the screws a little larger. You see the maintenance facility was in Chicago. They wore gloves during the cold winter months, and the head of the screws were too small to hold with their gloves.

How do you think that employee felt when management truly listened to his idea and reinforced it by saying, "That's a good idea. We will look at ways to implement it." Do you think he went back and shared this with all his buddies? I would venture to say it was the hot topic of conversation in the lunchroom for several weeks. I would also say that his buddies were now looking for ways to be more efficient in their respective jobs. Management must truly listen to the employees.

Communicate with your Employees

When was the last time you spoke to every one of your employees? Employees want to communicate with you. Open and honest communication with and from management will reinforce the importance of every employee within the organization. If your organization is relatively small, make it a point to learn a little something about everyone of your employees. Learn what they like to do. Learn their kid's names, and what they are involved in outside of work. You may be surprised. It may be a passion of theirs, and people love to talk about their passion. I can remember we had a mechanic at our production facility who did wood carvings of fish. His carvings were amazing. They looked so much like the real fish with each fin and scale carefully carved. Once I learned about his passion,

I would always ask him what he was currently working on. He would proudly bring the finished fish carvings into the plant to share them with everyone.

Another employee, Juanita, who ran the snack shop, refurbished and repaired old washing machines. She would sell them to employees who did not have a washing machine. So take a little interest in your employees. Find out what they do outside of work. This will go a long way in showing them that you care about them as individuals. It will show them that you do have their best interests in mind. Tap into the heart of your employees. Show them that you care. All that's required is for you to get to know them as people and not just employees.

A comprehensive internal communications program is a critical component of keeping employees engaged. Once again, as president, I would hold a monthly meeting with all of the office employees. I would share with them what I called the company vital signs, much like what the doctor checks for when you visit him. A physician's assistant does basically the same procedure every time prior to the doctor entering the exam room. They take your vital signs. They take your temperature, blood pressure and pulse and listen to your lungs with that cold stethoscope. During my monthly meeting, I would discuss the business vital signs. These included sales, expenses, and profitability versus both the budgeted and previous years' sales. I would also have the department managers share their successes within their respective departments. Whether it was a new customer, or a breakthrough in production efficiency, each manager, or at times, the employee responsible, would share their accomplishment or breakthrough. At these meetings, I would always reinforce the company's vision. I would also recognize the individuals who during the past month had contributed towards making our vision a reality.

I can remember once, standing on my desk in our open office area, announcing that we had just secured additional financing. Imagine what the employees thought when they saw me climb on the top of my desk and said, "Can I have your attention." Yes, we had an open office area. All of the desks were in a large open area without any walls or partitions. Everyone sat in the open area, including me. The open office was modeled after the open office environment at Mars, Inc.

Today communication can take a number of different forms. It can be something as outside the boundaries of ordinary thinking as standing on a desk. It can be email, company ezines, newsletters, or employee meetings, just to name a few.

Whirlpool provides a monthly recording called *"The Leaders Voice"* that each employee can dial in and listen to. It's a recorded message from senior leadership that updates company performance and business results. Whirlpool has also implemented an idea exchange program where employees can log into a company website. On the site they can exchange ideas and help find answers to questions they may have.

Management must continue to communicate even when sales are down or profits are poor. Employees need to know what's going on. The fear of the unknown is more detrimental to employee engagement than the sharing of poor performance. It could be just the rallying cry needed to drive the company ahead. You may be pleasantly surprised. The employees may have a suggestion that may be just what the company needs to improve performance. Be honest and upfront with your employees. If you do not know the answer to a question, let them know. But also let them know what you're going to do to find out the answer.

Communication does not always mean you're speaking. Being a good listener is also an important part of communicating, and management must be good listeners.

Good listening is more than hearing what the person you are talking with is saying. Good listening is trying to understand the intent and meaning of what is being said. Good listening is giving the speaker the opportunity to complete his or her thought without interruption. Good listening is focusing on the individual you are talking with and not letting your mind wander. It's not checking out of the conversation. It's acknowledging that the person you are talking with deserves your undivided attention.

Hire the Right Person

Hiring the right employees can have a major impact on your business. And don't be surprised if who you think is the right person for the job actually is not. Hiring the right person means hiring not only the person who can do the requirements of the job but who also has the skill set to do it well. This requires identifying the skills necessary to do the job. Certain individuals have a pre-disposition towards being *Fruitful Employees*. Businesses must make every effort to keep that pre-disposition in mind when hiring. Sometimes it's not who you think it is.

I have a good friend who a number of years ago owned a very successful rafting company. He had two major competitors in the market and both of these competitors were struggling for survival. As I was sharing the basic premise of the book, which all of you are very familiar with by now, he said Robert, "I now understand why my business was successful. We employed your *Thinking Beyond the Obvious* concept even though at the time we didn't know it." As I indicated in the introduction, many successful companies implement the strategy without even recognizing it.

Here's what Fred did in his company that differentiated his rafting business from his competitors. Most rafting companies, when they hire for the rafting season, hire experienced guides who know the river and who know how to negotiate the rapids. We are not talking Class 4 or higher extremely treacherous rapids. These experienced guides were usually somewhat reserved and their personalities reflected it. They were only interested in the trip down the river and not the total experience of the adventure. Contrary to what the majority of the rafting companies did, Fred's company hired outgoing, friendly individuals who loved pleasing people. They enjoyed serving others and insuring that their total rafting experience was exceptional. I asked Fred, "But they didn't know how to navigate the river?" His response was, *"We can train and teach them how to do that, but we can't teach them how to be friendly, outgoing individuals who want to help others."* The *Thinking Beyond the Obvious* concept that Fred recognized was not to do what every other rafting company was doing just because it seemed to be the right thing to do. Fred recognized what types of individuals he needed to hire to insure that the rafting experience was beyond expectations. Employees do make a difference. Making the right hire is just as important as engaging your employees.

Recognize Fruitful Employees

What absolutely amazes me is that 65% of Americans reported receiving no recognition for good work during the course of a year. This was reported in a recent Gallup Pole. Can you imagine that? Recognizing someone's efforts for a job well done is something that does not cost you anything, yet it is not regularly used as a management tool. Employees want to be recognized and rewarded for their contributions. Employees feel valued when management takes the time to recognize them for their contribution. Everyone wants to feel appreciated. It could be something as simple as saying, "Hey, great job on getting that rush order out. It sure helped solidify our relationship with a key customer." Not only did the employee receive recognition for a job well done, it also reinforced the connection between what the employee did and the goals of the business. Sometimes all that is needed are a few kind and encouraging words, and you'll make an employee's day. Sometimes as management you need to be a cheerleader, cheering on your employees to greater success and rewarding and recognizing the beyond the obvious activities that they do.

Save Mart supermarkets, a small grocery chain of 244 stores, primarily in California, started a tradition in 1952 that is still employed today. Save Mart uses mystery shoppers to grade all Save Mart stores four times per year. Each time a store scores exceptionally well, the names of all the employees of the particular store are placed in a hopper for a chance to win the annual employees-incentive prize. The prize could be cash or, as in some years, a new car. The CEO of Save Mart visits the store with the winning employee and presents the prize. In 2009, ten employees received $10,000 each.

Although, in this example, Save Mart didn't award individual performance, it did reward the efforts of the entire team.

This is not the first time the following has been written about, and I am sure this will not be the last, but T.E.A.M is the anagram for **T**ogether **E**veryone **A**chieves **M**ore. Employees need to recognize that they are part of the team. They must feel that the other members of the team are all contributing to the success of the business. They must feel that everyone, from the owners to the executives to the managers and the employees, are all working together for the good of the business.

This reminds me of a story I once heard of a man who was lost as he was driving through the country on a rainy day. As he tried to read the map, he veered off the road into the mud. Although he wasn't injured, his car was stuck in the mud. So the man walked to a nearby farmhouse to ask for help.

"Warwick can get you out of the mud," said a farmer pointing to an old mule standing in the field. The man looked at the farmer and then at the old mule and said, *"Well, I guess I have nothing to lose."* The two men and Warwick, the mule, made their way to the car.

The farmer hitched the mule to the car. With a snap of the reins the farmer shouted. *"Pull Fred! Pull Jack! Pull Ted! Pull Warwick."* And the mule pulled the car out of the mud with very little effort. He thanked the farmer, patted the mule and asked. *"Why did you call out all those other names before you called Warwick?"* The farmer grinned and said, *"Old Warwick is just about blind. As long as he believes he is part of a team, he doesn't mind pulling."* (Adapted from *Some Folks Feel the Rain … Others Just Get Wet.* James Moore, Dimensions).

CHAPTER EIGHT

Great-Grandmothers Do It Too

Kids do it, teenagers do it, young adults and mature adults alike do it, business professionals and blue-collar workers do it. My mom and my mother-in-law, who are both great-grandmothers, do it. You may be asking yourself. *"What is it that Great-Grandmothers do that I should be doing?"* They both have joined the Information Technology age and both use a computer. You may be also asking yourself. "Why is using a computer so significant? After all, doesn't everyone use a computer?"

It's not the use of a computer that is so significant. It's that both of these women have been open to and have welcomed innovation during their lifetimes. They've seen the reach of the telephone expand to penetrate a majority of the homes, and more recently they've seen the introduction and expansion of the cell phone. And during the last couple of years, they've also seen the introduction of video conferencing and both have used Skype™ the most popular type to talk with their great-grandchildren. They even got to see their newest great-grandbaby for the first time through Skype™ even though she was thousands of miles away.

And surprisingly they have both entered the computer age. It took quite a bit of pleading to convince my mom that her Royal typewriter was obsolete. I finally just gave her one of my old computers. My mom was totally amazed at what the computer did. I remember the first time I showed her how to use it. She was typing a form letter that the Spanish Club, of which she was secretary, would send to new members. As she was typing, a squiggly red line appeared under a word that she had just typed. Her response was, "Oh no, what did I do? I said, "Mom that's spell check. The computer will underline with a squiggly red line to let you know that you may have mistyped a word." I also told her that the computer would underline fragment sentences with a squiggly green line. She was absolutely amazed, when I showed her that she could save the letter and she would not have to retype it the next time she had to send it to a new member. She would only have to change the name. Her jaw dropped as she just sat their in awe.

So yes, great-grandmothers do it too. They use the technology available today.

Leverage Information Technology

The challenge facing businesses today is that technology is advancing at the speed of light. It's happening so quickly that no one can know everything and keep up with the changes. It's an absolute requirement that business owners, executives, and managers are technologically savvy, and that doesn't mean just keeping your computers up and running. Businesses today need to recognize that they operate at a frenetic pace. They need to recognize that transactions and decisions are essentially being made in real time. They must recognize that the use of information technology will help them transform their data into meaningful information. It will help them become more effective and more efficient.

Information Technology can be used in a number of different ways. The following are just a few examples. Information technology allows you to organize your data into useful information that can be used to track and measure your results, i.e., sales reports or inventory tracking reports. It allows you to target specific follow-up information to customers and prospects. It also enables you to minimize mistakes through process management and it enables you to engage your customers and prospects through permission marketing campaigns. Social media is also an important part of Information Technology.

Facebook, Twitter and LinkedIn, just to name a few, are tools that can be used to reach your prospects and customers.

I do not profess to be an expert in the realm of Information Technology, but I do know this: It's extremely important that you keep up with the rapid changes in the world of Information Technology. If great-grandmothers can use technology, you can too, and you should.

I would highly recommend that you seek out leading authorities on Information Technology through your local Chamber of Commerce. I would inquire if they have free workshops covering the subject. If your local Chamber of Commerce does not conduct such workshops, go on-line and search for Information Technology teleseminars or webinars. A webinar is an on-line seminar or conference that is accessed through your computer. Leading consultants and technology companies will conduct these as a way of gaining your contact information but they are very useful in learning what technologies are available today.

Do not fall behind. Be like the great-grandmothers who changed with the times. Use the technology available today.

CHAPTER NINE

A New Beginning

Congratulations. You have almost completed the book. But the book won't change your circumstances. Applying the *Thinking Beyond the Obvious* concept will.

Nolan Bushnell, the founder of Atari and Chuck E. Cheese's, said it best when he said, *"The critical ingredient is getting off your butt and doing something. It's as simple as that. A lot of people have ideas, but there are few who decide to do something about them now. Not tomorrow. Not next week. But today. The true entrepreneur is a doer, not a dreamer."*

Remember back to the beginning of the book. Remember my first *Thinking Beyond the Obvious* moment. By now you should all know what it means to *Think Beyond the Obvious,* to find those solutions that are outside the boundaries of ordinary thinking. I used that red Radio-Flyer wagon to haul buckets of tomatoes to the dumping station. Stop and think about what you learned in each chapter. From the first chapter, *"Picking Tomatoes",* to the last chapter *"Great Grandmothers Do It Too"* you learned what it means to think beyond the obvious. Example after example was used to illustrate the core concept. It's now time to apply what you've learned. It's now time to look at your business through your new, more discerning, *Thinking Beyond the Obvious* eyes.

But a word of caution, you can't do everything all at once. The easiest way to frustrate yourself and everyone around you is to try to implement everything discussed in this book immediately. At this point you have a number of new ideas to sift through and a number of ways you can make changes in your business. Start where you are right now. Reflect on the learnings from the various chapters and begin to implement what you have learned. Begin with the *"Are We There Yet?"* concept. Create your personal vision, followed by your business vision. After that is established in your business, it really doesn't matter which chapter you tackle next. Jack Nicklaus, one of the greatest golfers of all time, said it this way: *"Achievement is largely the product of steadily raising one's level of aspiration... and expectations."*

But as we finish up here, you will fall into one of three categories of the types of readers. The first type of reader will conclude that the concept doesn't apply to their business and will continue doing what they have always done. The difference is that this time they are hoping for different results.

The second group of readers will accept the basic concept but will not follow what was outlined in the *"Are We There Yet?"* chapter. They will not put together a plan of action that will help them achieve the results that they truly believe are possible.

And the last group of readers is the group that inspires me to continue to do what I love to do, to help business owner's position their business for success. These are the doers; they will seek to implement a plan of action. They will participate in the next *Thinking Beyond the Obvious Success Sessions* program. They will invest in transforming their business.

In the final analysis, it's important to realize that you are not alone. Countless business owners are struggling with what you're struggling with every day. But what separates you from the others is that you are taking action. Your first step was reading this book. Your next step will be applying what you have learned. And if you have trouble discerning how exactly to do it, I invite you to participate in the next *Thinking Beyond the Obvious Success Sessions* program.

The Success Session program is an eight-week Teleseminar series that will help you look at your business through new, awakened, and more discerning eyes. Each session will help you take what you have just read and teach you how to apply the concept to your individual business. Step-by-Step you will develop an intuitive understanding of how to position your business for success through the *Thinking Beyond the Obvious* concept.

Additional information can be found at:

www.ThinkingBeyondtheObvious.com

I hope you have enjoyed this book and I also hope it has inspired you to look for those solutions that are outside the boundaries of ordinary thinking—to position your business for success by, *"Thinking Beyond the Obvious"*

Now it's truly up to you to follow the words of the great football coach Vince Lombardi.

"It is time for us all to stand and cheer for the doer, the achiever—the one who recognizes the challenge and does something about it."

ABOUT THE AUTHOR

Robert **Mano** is a business consultant with experience that spans the spectrum from small businesses and startups to medium sized companies. He learned traditional marketing, sales, business and executive management at corporate giants Nestlé, Tenneco, Dole and Yorkshire Dried Fruit and Nut where he served as president. But more importantly, he experienced "real world" small business management while owning and operating 3 franchise sandwich shops.

Robert graduated from San Jose State University with a Bachelor of Arts Degree in Behavioral Science and completed additional course study in business, advertising, and marketing. He also completed a number of professional courses and seminars in the fields of sales, marketing, operations, and business management.

Taking the discipline of his corporate experience and coupling it with his small business ownership experience gives Robert a unique understanding of the problems and frustrations facing business owners today.

Robert founded Mano Y Mano Consulting in 2003 with the goal of positioning businesses for success. Robert uses a proprietary concept called *"Thinking Beyond the Obvious"* to help businesses reach their potential. *"Thinking Beyond the Obvious"* is a simple concept that drives business success.

> *"My passion is to use my past experiences to guide business owners through the maze of underachievement, confusion and misguided direction to position their businesses for success."*

Through his coaching/consulting, speaking engagements, training seminars and workshops, and published articles, Robert has instilled a renewed confidence and passion in those that own their own businesses.

BONUS

My gift to you for investing in your business and taking action is a 6 month trial subscription to the digital magazine "*Thinking Beyond the Obvious.*" (A $274.00 value)

This digital magazine will be delivered to your inbox each month, full of innovative ideas, insights and solutions that will position your business for success. It will have the feel of a physical magazine. You'll still be able to read and turn each page, but because it's digital, you'll also have access to outstanding videos and will be able to connect to important links.

The *Thinking Beyond the Obvious* Digital Magazine will include my own personal experiences as well as the writings and experiences of other leaders in the industry.

> "*Employ your time in improving yourself by other men's writings, so that you shall gain easily what others have labored hard for.*" *(Socrates)*

Each monthly issue will include a short introductory blog and a feature article written by me. But the magazine will also feature a guest article by some of the amazing people I have met throughout my career. Yes, I am going to tap into my own private network. Some of the articles may be business related, others may not. But they will all have one thing in common: each guest article will provide nuggets of wisdom that will enrich your lives (and very possibly your wallets.) You can choose to incorporate them or ignore them. The choice is entirely up to you. But I'm including them because I want to see each of you succeed and live your life to the fullest.

Each monthly issue will also include a blog post from Beth Bridges, *The Networking Motivator*™ and creator of the *Five Part Networking Success Plan*™. Beth is a leading networking expert (having attended more than 2000 networking events) and has entertained audiences throughout the U.S. with her simple innovative approach to a crucial business activity that many find daunting. Each month she will share stories, experiences, and advice that will help maximize your networking opportunities.

Lastly, each magazine will include inspirational quotes— words of wisdom that will help you stay on track, paint a magnificent picture in your mind of what's possible, and bring clarity to your vision. So carve a little time out of your busy schedule and take advantage of your six (6) month trial subscription to the *Thinking Beyond the Obvious* Digital Magazine. Go to www.thinkingbeyondtheobvious.com/dm and type in the word "success."

And remember, look for those solutions that are outside the boundaries of ordinary thinking. Drive your business success by *Thinking Beyond the Obvious*. It's what will differentiate your business from every other business in the market place.

CPSIA information can be obtained
at www.ICGtesting.com
Printed in the USA
JSHW052321280322
24340JS00001B/209